WWQT JOURNAL

WORLDWIDE QUIET TIME JOURNAL

WORLDWIDE QUITE TIME JOURNAL
Copyright © 2009 by ABWE Publications
Harrisburg, Pennsylvania 17105

Library of Congress Cataloging-in-Publications Data
(application pending)

ISBN-13: 978-1-888796-44-5

All Bible references are taken from the ESV.

Printed in the United States of America.

WWQT JOURNAL

WORLDWIDE QUIET TIME JOURNAL

JIM COOK

Association of Baptists for World Evangelism
P.O. Box 8585
Harrisburg, PA 17105–8585
(717) 774–7000
abwe@abwe.org

ABWE Canada
980 Adelaide St. South, Suite 34
London, Ontario N6E 1R3
(519) 690–1009
office@abwecanada.org

ABOUT THE AUTHOR

Jim Cook is the director of Next Generation Ministries, a ministry of the Association of Baptists for World Evangelism. Jim began a personal walk with Jesus Christ when he was a sailor in the US Navy. Some men from an organization called the Navigators showed him how to spend time alone with God. They called it a "quiet time." That stuck with Jim, and now he wants others to see the joy of seeking God and knowing Him personally. In his free time, Jim likes to play golf, especially when he can win against his two brothers.

ABOUT THE ARTISTS

Gary Varvel is the chief cartoonist for the *Indianapolis Star* editorial page. Gary is a committed believer in Jesus Christ and a deacon at his church. He teaches an adult Bible fellowship every Sunday. Gary's cartoon work has appeared in such international publications as *USA Today* and *World Magazine*.

Gary was assisted by his daughter, Ashley (Varvel) Day. Ashley is also a committed believer and, like her Dad, is also an artist. Together they are bringing their artwork to children around the world so that they can develop a personal walk with Jesus Christ.

WHY A WORLDWIDE QUIET TIME (WWQT) JOURNAL?

TO HELP YOU:

- Pray for all the countries of the world
- Seek God daily in His Word
- Grow in your time alone with God
- Journal your quiet time thoughts
- Learn about all the countries of the world
- Obey Scripture

Hebrews 11:6

"But without faith it is impossible to please Him.
For he that comes to God must believe that He is
and that He is a rewarder of them that diligently
seek Him."

Mark 11:17

"My house shall be called a house of prayer for
all the nations."

HOW TO USE YOUR WORLDWIDE QUIET TIME (WWQT) JOURNAL?

- Find a quiet place where there will be few or no interruptions. Ask your family to help you if you cannot find a place.
- Decide on a time to meet with God. Usually, morning is best. You can start the day out with God, learn from Him, and plan to obey Him.
- Bring your Bible, your WWQT Journal, and a pen. Anticipate God talking to you in His Word and listen for ways you can obey Him.
- Write down two things: what you learned and how you will obey. It is important to do both. The wise man who built his house on the rock heard the Word of God and obeyed.
- Share with others what you learned in your quiet time. Some will be happy to know that you are learning from God and trying to obey Him.

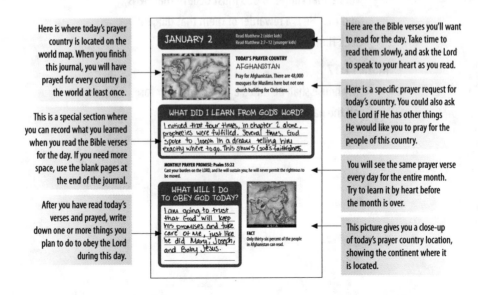

Here is where today's prayer country is located on the world map. When you finish this journal, you will have prayed for every country in the world at least once.

This is a special section where you can record what you learned when you read the Bible verses for the day. If you need more space, use the blank pages at the end of the journal.

After you have read today's verses and prayed, write down one or more things you plan to do to obey the Lord during this day.

Here are the Bible verses you'll want to read for the day. Take time to read them slowly, and ask the Lord to speak to your heart as you read.

Here is a specific prayer request for today's country. You could also ask the Lord if He has other things He would like you to pray for the people of this country.

You will see the same prayer verse every day for the entire month. Try to learn it by heart before the month is over.

This picture gives you a close-up of today's prayer country location, showing the continent where it is located.

Special thanks to Jenna Cook, the author's daughter, for filling in the handwritten sections of this sample page.

JANUARY 1

Read Matthew 1 (older kids)
Read Matthew 1:18–23 (younger kids)

TODAY'S PRAYER COUNTRY

AFGHANISTAN

Pray for Afghanistan. Ninety-nine out of one hundred people here do not believe that Jesus Christ is God.

WHAT DID I LEARN FROM GOD'S WORD?

_____

_____

_____

_____

MONTHLY PRAYER PROMISE: Psalm 55:22
Cast your burden on the LORD, and he will sustain you; he will never permit the righteous to be moved.

WHAT WILL I DO TO OBEY GOD TODAY?

_____

_____

_____

_____

_____

_____

FACT
The largest city in Afghanistan is Kabul, with over 2 million people.

JANUARY 2

Read Matthew 2 (older kids)
Read Matthew 2:7–12 (younger kids)

TODAY'S PRAYER COUNTRY

AFGHANISTAN

Pray for Afghanistan. There are 48,000 mosques for Muslims here but not one church building for Christians.

WHAT DID I LEARN FROM GOD'S WORD?

_____
_____
_____
_____

MONTHLY PRAYER PROMISE: Psalm 55:22
Cast your burden on the LORD, and he will sustain you; he will never permit the righteous to be moved.

WHAT WILL I DO TO OBEY GOD TODAY?

_____
_____
_____
_____
_____
_____
_____

ASIA

FACT
Only thirty-six percent of the people in Afghanistan can read.

JANUARY 3

Read Matthew 3:1–12 (older kids)
Read Matthew 3:1–5 (younger kids)

TODAY'S PRAYER COUNTRY

ALBANIA

Pray that many new people will be trained to lead the churches in Albania.

WHAT DID I LEARN FROM GOD'S WORD?

_____
_____
_____
_____

MONTHLY PRAYER PROMISE: Psalm 55:22
Cast your burden on the LORD, and he will sustain you; he will never permit the righteous to be moved.

WHAT WILL I DO TO OBEY GOD TODAY?

_____
_____
_____
_____
_____
_____
_____

EUROPE

FACT
Albania is slightly larger than the state of Maryland.

JANUARY 4

Read Matthew 3:13–17 (older kids)
Read Matthew 3:13–17 (younger kids)

TODAY'S PRAYER COUNTRY

ALBANIA

The ban on religion was lifted in 1990, but even now many people do not believe in Jesus Christ.

WHAT DID I LEARN FROM GOD'S WORD?

_____
_____
_____
_____

MONTHLY PRAYER PROMISE: Psalm 55:22
Cast your burden on the LORD, and he will sustain you; he will never permit the righteous to be moved.

WHAT WILL I DO TO OBEY GOD TODAY?

_____
_____
_____
_____
_____
_____

EUROPE

FACT
Albania is one of the poorest countries in Europe.

JANUARY 5

Read Matthew 4 (older kids)
Read Matthew 4:1–11 (younger kids)

TODAY'S PRAYER COUNTRY

ALGERIA

Almost the entire nation of Algeria is unreached and needs the Lord.

WHAT DID I LEARN FROM GOD'S WORD?

_____
_____
_____
_____

MONTHLY PRAYER PROMISE: Psalm 55:22
Cast your burden on the LORD, and he will sustain you; he will never permit the righteous to be moved.

WHAT WILL I DO TO OBEY GOD TODAY?

_____
_____
_____
_____
_____
_____
_____

AFRICA

FACT
The Sahara Desert covers about eighty-five percent of Algeria.

JANUARY 6

Read Matthew 5 (older kids)
Read Matthew 5:1–11 (younger kids)

TODAY'S PRAYER COUNTRY

ALGERIA

Pray for Arab believers who are being persecuted for their faith in Jesus Christ.

WHAT DID I LEARN FROM GOD'S WORD?

_____

_____

_____

_____

MONTHLY PRAYER PROMISE: Psalm 55:22
Cast your burden on the LORD, and he will sustain you; he will never permit the righteous to be moved.

WHAT WILL I DO TO OBEY GOD TODAY?

_____

_____

_____

_____

_____

_____

_____

AFRICA

FACT
About 100,000 people in Algeria have been killed by Islamic terrorists since 1992.

JANUARY 7

Read Matthew 6:1–15 (older kids)
Read Matthew 6:9–13 (younger kids)

TODAY'S PRAYER COUNTRY

AMERICAN SAMOA

Cults have taken a lot of people into their way of life. Pray for these people to come to Christ.

WHAT DID I LEARN FROM GOD'S WORD?

MONTHLY PRAYER PROMISE: Psalm 55:22
Cast your burden on the LORD, and he will sustain you; he will never permit the righteous to be moved.

WHAT WILL I DO TO OBEY GOD TODAY?

AUSTRALASIA

FACT
American Samoa has been a territory of the US since 1900.

JANUARY 8

Read Matthew 6:16–34 (older kids)
Read Matthew 6:28–34 (younger kids)

TODAY'S PRAYER COUNTRY

AMERICAN SAMOA

Pray for evangelistic churches to make an impact in their communities.

WHAT DID I LEARN FROM GOD'S WORD?

_____
_____
_____
_____

MONTHLY PRAYER PROMISE: Psalm 55:22
Cast your burden on the LORD, and he will sustain you; he will never permit the righteous to be moved.

WHAT WILL I DO TO OBEY GOD TODAY?

_____
_____
_____
_____
_____
_____
_____

AUSTRALASIA

FACT
American Samoa is made up of five volcanic islands and two coral atolls (ring-shaped islands surrounding a lagoon).

JANUARY 9

Read Matthew 7 (older kids)
Read Matthew 7:7–12 (younger kids)

TODAY'S PRAYER COUNTRY

ANDORRA

Having and caring a lot about possessions (sometimes called materialism) is very important here. Pray for people to see they need Christ.

WHAT DID I LEARN FROM GOD'S WORD?

_____
_____
_____
_____

MONTHLY PRAYER PROMISE: Psalm 55:22
Cast your burden on the LORD, and he will sustain you; he will never permit the righteous to be moved.

WHAT WILL I DO TO OBEY GOD TODAY?

_____
_____
_____
_____
_____
_____
_____

EUROPE

FACT
Andorra is a very small country located between France and Spain.

JANUARY 10

Read Matthew 8 (older kids)
Read Matthew 8:23–27 (younger kids)

TODAY'S PRAYER COUNTRY

ANDORRA

There are only a few Bible-preaching churches here. Pray for more churches to be started.

WHAT DID I LEARN FROM GOD'S WORD?

_____

_____

_____

_____

MONTHLY PRAYER PROMISE: Psalm 55:22
Cast your burden on the LORD, and he will sustain you; he will never permit the righteous to be moved.

WHAT WILL I DO TO OBEY GOD TODAY?

_____

_____

_____

_____

_____

_____

EUROPE

FACT
About 75,000 people live in Andorra.

JANUARY 11

Read Matthew 9:1–17 (older kids)
Read Matthew 9:9–13 (younger kids)

TODAY'S PRAYER COUNTRY

ANGOLA

The country of Angola has been at war most of the time since 1962. Pray for these people to know the Prince of Peace.

WHAT DID I LEARN FROM GOD'S WORD?

_____

_____

_____

_____

MONTHLY PRAYER PROMISE: Psalm 55:22
Cast your burden on the LORD, and he will sustain you; he will never permit the righteous to be moved.

WHAT WILL I DO TO OBEY GOD TODAY?

_____

_____

_____

_____

_____

_____

AFRICA

FACT
Angola is more than three times the size of California.

JANUARY 12

Read Matthew 9:18–38 (older kids)
Read Matthew 9:35–38 (younger kids)

TODAY'S PRAYER COUNTRY
ANGOLA

The first president of Angola promised to get rid of Christianity there within twenty years. Pray for persecuted Christians.

WHAT DID I LEARN FROM GOD'S WORD?

_____

_____

_____

_____

MONTHLY PRAYER PROMISE: Psalm 55:22
Cast your burden on the LORD, and he will sustain you; he will never permit the righteous to be moved.

WHAT WILL I DO TO OBEY GOD TODAY?

_____

_____

_____

_____

_____

_____

_____

AFRICA

FACT
Angola was a Portuguese colony for 450 years. It became independent in 1975.

JANUARY 13

Read Matthew 10:1–42 (older kids)
Read Matthew 10:1–7 (younger kids)

TODAY'S PRAYER COUNTRY

ANGUILLA

There is not much evangelism going on in Anguilla. Pray for more efforts to take the gospel to the lost there.

WHAT DID I LEARN FROM GOD'S WORD?

_____
_____
_____
_____

MONTHLY PRAYER PROMISE: Psalm 55:22
Cast your burden on the LORD, and he will sustain you; he will never permit the righteous to be moved.

WHAT WILL I DO TO OBEY GOD TODAY?

_____
_____
_____
_____
_____
_____

NORTH AMERICA

FACT
Anguilla is located in the Caribbean Sea and is the most northern of the Leeward Islands.

JANUARY 14

Read Matthew 11:1–19 (older kids)
Read Matthew 11:7–15 (younger kids)

TODAY'S PRAYER COUNTRY
ANGUILLA

When people here come to Christ, efforts to disciple them are very limited. Pray for converts to be discipled.

WHAT DID I LEARN FROM GOD'S WORD?

_____
_____
_____
_____

MONTHLY PRAYER PROMISE: Psalm 55:22
Cast your burden on the LORD, and he will sustain you; he will never permit the righteous to be moved.

WHAT WILL I DO TO OBEY GOD TODAY?

_____
_____
_____
_____
_____
_____
_____

NORTH AMERICA

FACT
The economy of Anguilla depends heavily on tourism.

JANUARY 15

Read Matthew 11:20–30 (older kids)
Read Matthew 11:28–30 (younger kids)

TODAY'S PRAYER COUNTRY

ANTIGUA AND BARBUDA

Drug-dealing, violence, and gambling are common here. Pray for people to be convicted of these sins.

WHAT DID I LEARN FROM GOD'S WORD?

_____
_____
_____
_____

MONTHLY PRAYER PROMISE: Psalm 55:22
Cast your burden on the LORD, and he will sustain you; he will never permit the righteous to be moved.

WHAT WILL I DO TO OBEY GOD TODAY?

_____
_____
_____
_____
_____
_____

NORTH AMERICA

FACT
Antigua and Barbuda are islands in the Caribbean Sea. Antigua is almost twice as big as Barbuda.

JANUARY 16

Read Matthew 12 (older kids)
Read Matthew 12:46–50 (younger kids)

TODAY'S PRAYER COUNTRY

ANTIGUA AND BARBUDA

Pray for Christians here to experience revival. Many are content not to grow in their commitment to Jesus Christ.

WHAT DID I LEARN FROM GOD'S WORD?

_____
_____
_____
_____

MONTHLY PRAYER PROMISE: Psalm 55:22
Cast your burden on the LORD, and he will sustain you; he will never permit the righteous to be moved.

WHAT WILL I DO TO OBEY GOD TODAY?

_____
_____
_____
_____
_____
_____
_____

NORTH AMERICA

FACT
Antigua was explored by Christopher Columbus in 1493.

JANUARY 17

Read Matthew 13:1–23 (older kids)
Read Matthew 13:18–23 (younger kids)

TODAY'S PRAYER COUNTRY

ARGENTINA

Pray for laborers to enter the spiritual harvest fields of Argentina.

WHAT DID I LEARN FROM GOD'S WORD?

_____

_____

_____

_____

MONTHLY PRAYER PROMISE: Psalm 55:22
Cast your burden on the LORD, and he will sustain you; he will never permit the righteous to be moved.

WHAT WILL I DO TO OBEY GOD TODAY?

_____

_____

_____

_____

_____

_____

FACT
In South America, Argentina is second in size and population to Brazil.

JANUARY 18

Read Matthew 13:24–58 (older kids)
Read Matthew 13:53–58 (younger kids)

TODAY'S PRAYER COUNTRY

ARGENTINA

Economic problems have caused hardship in Argentina. Pray for God to use these problems to bring people to Him.

WHAT DID I LEARN FROM GOD'S WORD?

_____
_____
_____
_____

MONTHLY PRAYER PROMISE: Psalm 55:22
Cast your burden on the LORD, and he will sustain you; he will never permit the righteous to be moved.

WHAT WILL I DO TO OBEY GOD TODAY?

_____
_____
_____
_____
_____
_____
_____

SOUTH AMERICA

FACT
Aconcagua, a mountain in Argentina, is the highest mountain in the world outside of Asia.

JANUARY 19

Read Matthew 14:1–21 (older kids)
Read Matthew 14:13–21 (younger kids)

TODAY'S PRAYER COUNTRY

ARMENIA

Pray that Armenian Christians will be a source of spiritual light to surrounding nations.

WHAT DID I LEARN FROM GOD'S WORD?

MONTHLY PRAYER PROMISE: Psalm 55:22
Cast your burden on the LORD, and he will sustain you; he will never permit the righteous to be moved.

WHAT WILL I DO TO OBEY GOD TODAY?

FACT
Armenia is a land full of rugged mountains and extinct volcanoes.

JANUARY 20

Read Matthew 14:22–36 (older kids)
Read Matthew 14:25–32 (younger kids)

TODAY'S PRAYER COUNTRY

ARMENIA

Pray for resources to train the leadership of the Armenian churches.

WHAT DID I LEARN FROM GOD'S WORD?

_____
_____
_____
_____

MONTHLY PRAYER PROMISE: Psalm 55:22
Cast your burden on the LORD, and he will sustain you; he will never permit the righteous to be moved.

WHAT WILL I DO TO OBEY GOD TODAY?

_____
_____
_____
_____
_____
_____

FACT
Armenia was the first country in the world to officially embrace Christianity (300 AD).

JANUARY 21

Read Matthew 15:1–20 (older kids)
Read Matthew 15:3–8 (younger kids)

TODAY'S PRAYER COUNTRY

ARUBA

Christian radio programs are broadcast into Aruba every day. Pray for spiritual fruit from this ministry.

WHAT DID I LEARN FROM GOD'S WORD?

_____
_____
_____
_____

MONTHLY PRAYER PROMISE: Psalm 55:22
Cast your burden on the LORD, and he will sustain you; he will never permit the righteous to be moved.

WHAT WILL I DO TO OBEY GOD TODAY?

_____
_____
_____
_____
_____
_____
_____

SOUTH AMERICA

FACT
Aruba is an island slightly larger than Washington, D.C.

JANUARY 22

Read Matthew 15:21–39 (older kids)
Read Matthew 15:32–39 (younger kids)

TODAY'S PRAYER COUNTRY

ARUBA

Four out of five Arubans are Roman Catholic and believe that you have to do good things to get to heaven. Pray for them.

WHAT DID I LEARN FROM GOD'S WORD?

_____
_____
_____
_____

MONTHLY PRAYER PROMISE: Psalm 55:22
Cast your burden on the LORD, and he will sustain you; he will never permit the righteous to be moved.

WHAT WILL I DO TO OBEY GOD TODAY?

_____
_____
_____
_____
_____
_____

SOUTH AMERICA

FACT
The Netherlands controls Aruba's defense and foreign affairs.

JANUARY 23

Read Matthew 16 (older kids)
Read Matthew 16:13–20 (younger kids)

TODAY'S PRAYER COUNTRY
AUSTRALIA

There is much emphasis in Australia on enjoying pleasure and gaining wealth. Pray for Australians to turn to God.

WHAT DID I LEARN FROM GOD'S WORD?

_____
_____
_____
_____

MONTHLY PRAYER PROMISE: Psalm 55:22
Cast your burden on the LORD, and he will sustain you; he will never permit the righteous to be moved.

WHAT WILL I DO TO OBEY GOD TODAY?

_____
_____
_____
_____
_____
_____
_____

AUSTRALASIA

FACT
Australia is about the same size as the United States would be without Alaska and Hawaii.

JANUARY 24

Read Matthew 17 (older kids)
Read Matthew 17:1–5 (younger kids)

TODAY'S PRAYER COUNTRY
AUSTRALIA
Church attendance in Australia has been declining steadily. Pray for churches to grow.

WHAT DID I LEARN FROM GOD'S WORD?

_____
_____
_____
_____

MONTHLY PRAYER PROMISE: Psalm 55:22
Cast your burden on the LORD, and he will sustain you; he will never permit the righteous to be moved.

WHAT WILL I DO TO OBEY GOD TODAY?

_____
_____
_____
_____
_____
_____

AUSTRALASIA

FACT
When Captain James Cook landed on Australia in 1770, he claimed it for the British.

JANUARY 25

Read Matthew 18:1–14 (older kids)
Read Matthew 18:10–14 (younger kids)

TODAY'S PRAYER COUNTRY

AUSTRIA

Pray for Austria, a cultured country known for its music and art. The Austrians need a personal faith in Christ.

WHAT DID I LEARN FROM GOD'S WORD?

MONTHLY PRAYER PROMISE: Psalm 55:22
Cast your burden on the LORD, and he will sustain you; he will never permit the righteous to be moved.

WHAT WILL I DO TO OBEY GOD TODAY?

EUROPE

FACT
The voting age in Austria is sixteen.

JANUARY 26

Read Matthew 18:15–35 (older kids)
Read Matthew 18:15–20 (younger kids)

TODAY'S PRAYER COUNTRY

AUSTRIA

Very few Austrians go into full-time Christian service and missionary work. Pray for more Austrians to allow the Lord to use them in this way.

WHAT DID I LEARN FROM GOD'S WORD?

_____
_____
_____
_____

MONTHLY PRAYER PROMISE: Psalm 55:22
Cast your burden on the LORD, and he will sustain you; he will never permit the righteous to be moved.

WHAT WILL I DO TO OBEY GOD TODAY?

_____
_____
_____
_____
_____
_____
_____

EUROPE

FACT
The Alps cover about seventy percent of Austria.

JANUARY 27

Read Matthew 19 (older kids)
Read Matthew 19:13–14 (younger kids)

TODAY'S PRAYER COUNTRY
AZERBAIJAN

Pray for the many homeless and unemployed refugees who live in Azerbaijan.

WHAT DID I LEARN FROM GOD'S WORD?

_____
_____
_____
_____

MONTHLY PRAYER PROMISE: Psalm 55:22
Cast your burden on the LORD, and he will sustain you; he will never permit the righteous to be moved.

WHAT WILL I DO TO OBEY GOD TODAY?

_____
_____
_____
_____
_____
_____
_____

ASIA

FACT
Azerbaijan has untapped oil resources worth trillions of dollars.

JANUARY 28

Read Matthew 20 (older kids)
Read Matthew 20:20–28 (younger kids)

TODAY'S PRAYER COUNTRY

AZERBAIJAN

Most of the Azerbaijani towns and villages have never been evangelized. Pray for these towns and villages.

WHAT DID I LEARN FROM GOD'S WORD?

_____
_____
_____
_____

MONTHLY PRAYER PROMISE: Psalm 55:22
Cast your burden on the LORD, and he will sustain you; he will never permit the righteous to be moved.

WHAT WILL I DO TO OBEY GOD TODAY?

_____
_____
_____
_____
_____
_____
_____

FACT
The largest city in Azerbaijan is Baku, with over 2 million people.

JANUARY 29

Read Matthew 21 (older kids)
Read Matthew 21:6–11 (younger kids)

TODAY'S PRAYER COUNTRY
BAHAMAS

Money from drug dealing has negatively affected the culture here. Pray for changes that glorify God.

WHAT DID I LEARN FROM GOD'S WORD?

_____
_____
_____
_____

MONTHLY PRAYER PROMISE: Psalm 55:22
Cast your burden on the LORD, and he will sustain you; he will never permit the righteous to be moved.

WHAT WILL I DO TO OBEY GOD TODAY?

_____
_____
_____
_____
_____
_____
_____

NORTH AMERICA

FACT
The Bahamas consist of about 700 islands.

JANUARY 30

Read Matthew 22 (older kids)
Read Matthew 22:34–40 (younger kids)

TODAY'S PRAYER COUNTRY

BAHAMAS

Pray for revival and a vision for missions among believers.

WHAT DID I LEARN FROM GOD'S WORD?

_____
_____
_____
_____

MONTHLY PRAYER PROMISE: Psalm 55:22
Cast your burden on the LORD, and he will sustain you; he will never permit the righteous to be moved.

WHAT WILL I DO TO OBEY GOD TODAY?

_____
_____
_____
_____
_____
_____
_____

NORTH AMERICA

FACT
People can live on only thirty of these islands.

JANUARY 31

Read Matthew 23:1–22 (older kids)
Read Matthew 23:1–11 (younger kids)

TODAY'S PRAYER COUNTRY

BAHRAIN

The largest Arab Christian community is here in the gulf states. Pray for these believers as they share Jesus Christ.

WHAT DID I LEARN FROM GOD'S WORD?

_____

_____

_____

_____

MONTHLY PRAYER PROMISE: Psalm 55:22
Cast your burden on the LORD, and he will sustain you; he will never permit the righteous to be moved.

WHAT WILL I DO TO OBEY GOD TODAY?

_____

_____

_____

_____

_____

_____

ASIA

FACT
Bahrain means "two seas" and is located between Saudi Arabia and Qatar.

FEBRUARY 1

Read Matthew 23:23–39 (older kids)
Read Matthew 23:37–39 (younger kids)

TODAY'S PRAYER COUNTRY

BAHRAIN

Pray for continued religious freedom in Bahrain.

WHAT DID I LEARN FROM GOD'S WORD?

_____
_____
_____
_____

MONTHLY PRAYER PROMISE: John 16:24
Until now you have asked nothing in my name. Ask, and you will receive, that your joy may be full.

WHAT WILL I DO TO OBEY GOD TODAY?

_____
_____
_____
_____
_____
_____
_____

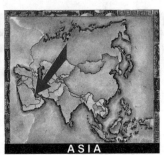

ASIA

FACT
Bahrain gained full independence from Great Britain in 1971.

FEBRUARY 2

Read Matthew 24 (older kids)
Read Matthew 24:42–51 (younger kids)

TODAY'S PRAYER COUNTRY

BANGLADESH

Pray for a continued openness to the gospel despite increased Islamic pressure.

WHAT DID I LEARN FROM GOD'S WORD?

_____
_____
_____
_____

MONTHLY PRAYER PROMISE: John 16:24
Until now you have asked nothing in my name. Ask, and you will receive, that your joy may be full.

WHAT WILL I DO TO OBEY GOD TODAY?

_____
_____
_____
_____
_____
_____

ASIA

FACT
Tropical monsoons and frequent floods cause heavy damage in many areas of Bangladesh.

FEBRUARY 3

Read Matthew 25 (older kids)
Read Matthew 25:36–40 (younger kids)

TODAY'S PRAYER COUNTRY

BANGLADESH

Pray for the many people here who experience poverty and suffering.

WHAT DID I LEARN FROM GOD'S WORD?

_____
_____
_____
_____

MONTHLY PRAYER PROMISE: John 16:24
Until now you have asked nothing in my name. Ask, and you will receive, that your joy may be full.

WHAT WILL I DO TO OBEY GOD TODAY?

_____
_____
_____
_____
_____
_____
_____

ASIA

FACT
Before 1971, when the people fought a war for independence, Bangladesh was known as East Pakistan.

FEBRUARY 4

Read Matthew 26:1–46 (older kids)
Read Matthew 26:36–46 (younger kids)

TODAY'S PRAYER COUNTRY
BARBADOS

Young people here need good role models who demonstrate how to live for Jesus Christ. Pray for God to give them such role models.

WHAT DID I LEARN FROM GOD'S WORD?

_____
_____
_____
_____

MONTHLY PRAYER PROMISE: John 16:24
Until now you have asked nothing in my name. Ask, and you will receive, that your joy may be full.

WHAT WILL I DO TO OBEY GOD TODAY?

_____
_____
_____
_____
_____
_____
_____

SOUTH AMERICA

FACT
Barbados gained its independence from Great Britain in 1966.

FEBRUARY 5

Read Matthew 26:47–75 (older kids)
Read Matthew 26:69–75 (younger kids)

TODAY'S PRAYER COUNTRY

BARBADOS

The missions vision of Barbados is very limited. Pray for God to send out missionaries from Barbados.

WHAT DID I LEARN FROM GOD'S WORD?

_____

_____

_____

_____

MONTHLY PRAYER PROMISE: John 16:24
Until now you have asked nothing in my name. Ask, and you will receive, that your joy may be full.

WHAT WILL I DO TO OBEY GOD TODAY?

_____

_____

_____

_____

_____

_____

SOUTH AMERICA

FACT
Slavery in Barbados was abolished in 1834.

FEBRUARY 6

Read Matthew 27:1–31 (older kids)
Read Matthew 27:27–31 (younger kids)

TODAY'S PRAYER COUNTRY
BELGIUM

About ninety percent of the people who live in Belgium claim to be Roman Catholic. Pray for them to come to Jesus Christ.

WHAT DID I LEARN FROM GOD'S WORD?

_____
_____
_____
_____

MONTHLY PRAYER PROMISE: John 16:24
Until now you have asked nothing in my name. Ask, and you will receive, that your joy may be full.

WHAT WILL I DO TO OBEY GOD TODAY?

_____
_____
_____
_____
_____
_____
_____

EUROPE

FACT
This area was conquered by Julius Caesar in 57–50 B.C.

FEBRUARY 7

TODAY'S PRAYER COUNTRY

BELGIUM

Spiritually, Belgium is one of the neediest countries in Europe. Pray that these spiritual needs will be met.

WHAT DID I LEARN FROM GOD'S WORD?

_____
_____
_____
_____

MONTHLY PRAYER PROMISE: John 16:24
Until now you have asked nothing in my name. Ask, and you will receive, that your joy may be full.

WHAT WILL I DO TO OBEY GOD TODAY?

_____
_____
_____
_____
_____
_____
_____

EUROPE

FACT
Brussels, the capital of Belgium, is the hub for many European Union (EU) financial activities.

FEBRUARY 8

Read Matthew 28 (older kids)
Read Matthew 28:16–20 (younger kids)

TODAY'S PRAYER COUNTRY

BELIZE

There are very few full-time Christian workers in Belize. Pray for the churches to be able to support their pastors.

WHAT DID I LEARN FROM GOD'S WORD?

_____
_____
_____
_____

MONTHLY PRAYER PROMISE: John 16:24
Until now you have asked nothing in my name. Ask, and you will receive, that your joy may be full.

WHAT WILL I DO TO OBEY GOD TODAY?

_____
_____
_____
_____
_____
_____
_____

NORTH AMERICA

FACT
Belize is about the size of New Hampshire.

FEBRUARY 9

Read Mark 1 (older kids)
Read Mark 1:35–39 (younger kids)

TODAY'S PRAYER COUNTRY
BELIZE

In Belize, there is a lot of evangelism but not much follow-up or discipleship. Pray for these efforts.

WHAT DID I LEARN FROM GOD'S WORD?

_____
_____
_____
_____

MONTHLY PRAYER PROMISE: John 16:24
Until now you have asked nothing in my name. Ask, and you will receive, that your joy may be full.

WHAT WILL I DO TO OBEY GOD TODAY?

_____
_____
_____
_____
_____
_____
_____

NORTH AMERICA

FACT
European contact with this area began in 1502, when Columbus sailed along the coast.

FEBRUARY 10

Read Mark 2:1–17 (older kids)
Read Mark 2:1–5 (younger kids)

TODAY'S PRAYER COUNTRY
BENIN

There is not much being done to evangelize the lost here, even though Benin is not a Muslim majority country. Please pray more will be done.

WHAT DID I LEARN FROM GOD'S WORD?

MONTHLY PRAYER PROMISE: John 16:24
Until now you have asked nothing in my name. Ask, and you will receive, that your joy may be full.

WHAT WILL I DO TO OBEY GOD TODAY?

AFRICA

FACT
Benin is a hot and humid country.

FEBRUARY 11

Read Mark 2:18–28 (older kids)
Read Mark 2:23–28 (younger kids)

TODAY'S PRAYER COUNTRY

BENIN

About one out of every five people who live here are Muslim. Pray for them.

WHAT DID I LEARN FROM GOD'S WORD?

MONTHLY PRAYER PROMISE: John 16:24
Until now you have asked nothing in my name. Ask, and you will receive, that your joy may be full.

WHAT WILL I DO TO OBEY GOD TODAY?

AFRICA

FACT
Less than half of the people in Benin can read.

FEBRUARY 12

Read Mark 3 (older kids)
Read Mark 3:31–35 (younger kids)

TODAY'S PRAYER COUNTRY

BHUTAN

The people of Bhutan are almost all Buddhist and know very little or nothing about Jesus Christ. Pray for them to hear the Good News.

WHAT DID I LEARN FROM GOD'S WORD?

_____

_____

_____

_____

MONTHLY PRAYER PROMISE: John 16:24
Until now you have asked nothing in my name. Ask, and you will receive, that your joy may be full.

WHAT WILL I DO TO OBEY GOD TODAY?

_____

_____

_____

_____

_____

_____

FACT
Bhutan is located very close to the Himalaya Mountains.

FEBRUARY 13

Read Mark 4:1–20 (older kids)
Read Mark 4:1–9 (younger kids)

TODAY'S PRAYER COUNTRY
BOLIVIA

Pray that believers in Bolivia will be unified as they reach out to the lost in this country.

WHAT DID I LEARN FROM GOD'S WORD?

_____
_____
_____
_____

MONTHLY PRAYER PROMISE: John 16:24
Until now you have asked nothing in my name. Ask, and you will receive, that your joy may be full.

WHAT WILL I DO TO OBEY GOD TODAY?

_____
_____
_____
_____
_____
_____
_____

SOUTH AMERICA

FACT
Lake Titicaca is the highest lake in the world on which you can travel by boat.

FEBRUARY 14

Read Mark 4:21–41 (older kids)
Read Mark 4:35–41 (younger kids)

TODAY'S PRAYER COUNTRY

BOLIVIA

Pray that Bolivians would come to Jesus Christ and not rely on superstitions and magic.

WHAT DID I LEARN FROM GOD'S WORD?

_____
_____
_____
_____

MONTHLY PRAYER PROMISE: John 16:24
Until now you have asked nothing in my name. Ask, and you will receive, that your joy may be full.

WHAT WILL I DO TO OBEY GOD TODAY?

_____
_____
_____
_____
_____
_____
_____

SOUTH AMERICA

FACT
The capital, La Paz, is the highest capital city in the world at 11,910 feet.

FEBRUARY 15

Read Mark 5 (older kids)
Read Mark 5:1–13 (younger kids)

TODAY'S PRAYER COUNTRY

BOSNIA AND HERZEGOVINA

War has torn this country apart. Pray for the people of Bosnia and Herzegovina to know the Prince of Peace.

WHAT DID I LEARN FROM GOD'S WORD?

_____
_____
_____
_____

MONTHLY PRAYER PROMISE: John 16:24
Until now you have asked nothing in my name. Ask, and you will receive, that your joy may be full.

WHAT WILL I DO TO OBEY GOD TODAY?

_____
_____
_____
_____
_____
_____
_____

EUROPE

FACT
The capital city, Sarajevo, hosted the 1984 Winter Olympics.

FEBRUARY 16

Read Mark 6 (older kids)
Read Mark 6:7–13 (younger kids)

TODAY'S PRAYER COUNTRY

BOSNIA AND HERZEGOVINA

Pray for all the Roma people (formerly called Gypsies) who need Jesus.

WHAT DID I LEARN FROM GOD'S WORD?

_____
_____
_____
_____

MONTHLY PRAYER PROMISE: John 16:24
Until now you have asked nothing in my name. Ask, and you will receive, that your joy may be full.

WHAT WILL I DO TO OBEY GOD TODAY?

_____
_____
_____
_____
_____
_____

EUROPE

FACT
Almost half of the Bosnians do not have jobs.

FEBRUARY 17

Read Mark 7:1–23 (older kids)
Read Mark 7:6–13 (younger kids)

TODAY'S PRAYER COUNTRY
BOTSWANA

AIDS has become a terrible problem for people in Botswana. Pray for those who are affected by this disease.

WHAT DID I LEARN FROM GOD'S WORD?

_____
_____
_____
_____

MONTHLY PRAYER PROMISE: John 16:24
Until now you have asked nothing in my name. Ask, and you will receive, that your joy may be full.

WHAT WILL I DO TO OBEY GOD TODAY?

_____
_____
_____
_____
_____
_____

FACT
The official language of Botswana is English, but only two out of 100 speak it.

FEBRUARY 18

Read Mark 7:24–37 (older kids)
Read Mark 7:24–30 (younger kids)

TODAY'S PRAYER COUNTRY

BOTSWANA

Pray for Biblical training to be provided for the church leaders in Botswana.

WHAT DID I LEARN FROM GOD'S WORD?

_____

_____

_____

_____

MONTHLY PRAYER PROMISE: John 16:24
Until now you have asked nothing in my name. Ask, and you will receive, that your joy may be full.

WHAT WILL I DO TO OBEY GOD TODAY?

_____

_____

_____

_____

_____

_____

_____

FACT
Botswana gained independence from Great Britain in 1965.

FEBRUARY 19

Read Mark 8 (older kids)
Read Mark 8:1–10 (younger kids)

TODAY'S PRAYER COUNTRY

BRAZIL

Many missionaries in Brazil are using sports for outreach. Pray for people to come to Christ.

WHAT DID I LEARN FROM GOD'S WORD?

_____
_____
_____
_____

MONTHLY PRAYER PROMISE: John 16:24
Until now you have asked nothing in my name. Ask, and you will receive, that your joy may be full.

WHAT WILL I DO TO OBEY GOD TODAY?

_____
_____
_____
_____
_____
_____
_____

SOUTH AMERICA

FACT
Brazil is the largest South American country, both in size and population.

FEBRUARY 20

Read Mark 9:1–29 (older kids)
Read Mark 9:2–13 (younger kids)

TODAY'S PRAYER COUNTRY

BRAZIL

Pray for more Brazilian church planters.

WHAT DID I LEARN FROM GOD'S WORD?

_____
_____
_____
_____

MONTHLY PRAYER PROMISE: John 16:24
Until now you have asked nothing in my name. Ask, and you will receive, that your joy may
be full.

WHAT WILL I DO
TO OBEY GOD TODAY?

_____
_____
_____
_____
_____
_____
_____

SOUTH AMERICA

FACT
The people in Brazil speak mostly
Portuguese.

FEBRUARY 21

Read Mark 9:30–50 (older kids)
Read Mark 9:38–41 (younger kids)

TODAY'S PRAYER COUNTRY
BRUNEI

Many Muslims here do not want any Christians in Brunei. Pray for people to come to Christ.

WHAT DID I LEARN FROM GOD'S WORD?

_____
_____
_____
_____

MONTHLY PRAYER PROMISE: John 16:24
Until now you have asked nothing in my name. Ask, and you will receive, that your joy may be full.

WHAT WILL I DO TO OBEY GOD TODAY?

_____
_____
_____
_____
_____
_____

AUSTRALASIA

FACT
Brunei is about the size of Delaware and is located on the island of Borneo.

FEBRUARY 22

Read Mark 10 (older kids)
Read Mark 10:13–16 (younger kids)

TODAY'S PRAYER COUNTRY

BULGARIA

There is more spiritual freedom in Bulgaria than there used to be. Pray for God to use this openness for His glory.

WHAT DID I LEARN FROM GOD'S WORD?

MONTHLY PRAYER PROMISE: John 16:24
Until now you have asked nothing in my name. Ask, and you will receive, that your joy may be full.

WHAT WILL I DO TO OBEY GOD TODAY?

EUROPE

FACT
Bulgaria is about the same size as the state of Tennessee.

FEBRUARY 23

Read Mark 11 (older kids)
Read Mark 11:1–11 (younger kids)

TODAY'S PRAYER COUNTRY

BULGARIA

Missionaries have had a hard time staying in Bulgaria. Pray for more missionaries to stay and help.

WHAT DID I LEARN FROM GOD'S WORD?

MONTHLY PRAYER PROMISE: John 16:24
Until now you have asked nothing in my name. Ask, and you will receive, that your joy may be full.

WHAT WILL I DO TO OBEY GOD TODAY?

EUROPE

FACT
The famous Danube River flows through Bulgaria, but it is not the main river in this country.

FEBRUARY 24

Read Mark 12:1–27 (older kids)
Read Mark 12:1–11 (younger kids)

TODAY'S PRAYER COUNTRY

BURKINA FASO

The people here have few or no Christian resources available to them. Pray for them to hear God's Word.

WHAT DID I LEARN FROM GOD'S WORD?

_____
_____
_____
_____

MONTHLY PRAYER PROMISE: John 16:24
Until now you have asked nothing in my name. Ask, and you will receive, that your joy may be full.

WHAT WILL I DO TO OBEY GOD TODAY?

_____
_____
_____
_____
_____
_____
_____

AFRICA

FACT
The capital city is Ouagadougou, which has about 1 million people.

FEBRUARY 25

Read Mark 12:28–44 (older kids)
Read Mark 12:28–34 (younger kids)

TODAY'S PRAYER COUNTRY
BURUNDI

The Hutu and the Tutsi peoples do not like each other at all. Pray for them to receive the love of Jesus Christ.

WHAT DID I LEARN FROM GOD'S WORD?

MONTHLY PRAYER PROMISE: John 16:24
Until now you have asked nothing in my name. Ask, and you will receive, that your joy may be full.

WHAT WILL I DO TO OBEY GOD TODAY?

AFRICA

FACT
The people who live here are mostly Hutu (eighty-five percent) or Tutsi (fourteen percent).

FEBRUARY 26

Read Mark 13 (older kids)
Read Mark 13:32–37 (younger kids)

TODAY'S PRAYER COUNTRY

CAMBODIA

Because of cruel things that were done to them, many people here have learned to hate. Pray for them to know the love of Jesus Christ.

WHAT DID I LEARN FROM GOD'S WORD?

MONTHLY PRAYER PROMISE: John 16:24
Until now you have asked nothing in my name. Ask, and you will receive, that your joy may be full.

WHAT WILL I DO TO OBEY GOD TODAY?

ASIA

FACT
As many as 2 million Cambodians were killed during a war several years ago.

FEBRUARY 27

Read Mark 14 (older kids)
Read Mark 14:22–31 (younger kids)

TODAY'S PRAYER COUNTRY

CAMBODIA

Pray for the children of Cambodia. One or more of every three children here are abused.

WHAT DID I LEARN FROM GOD'S WORD?

_____
_____
_____
_____

MONTHLY PRAYER PROMISE: John 16:24
Until now you have asked nothing in my name. Ask, and you will receive, that your joy may be full.

WHAT WILL I DO TO OBEY GOD TODAY?

_____
_____
_____
_____
_____
_____
_____

FACT
Ninety-five percent of the people in Cambodia are Buddhist.

FEBRUARY 28

Read Mark 15:1–20 (older kids)
Read Mark 15:16–20 (younger kids)

TODAY'S PRAYER COUNTRY
CAMEROON

Cameroon is a country where many people are not serving God. Pray for these people to learn the truth of Jesus Christ.

WHAT DID I LEARN FROM GOD'S WORD?

_____
_____
_____
_____

MONTHLY PRAYER PROMISE: John 16:24
Until now you have asked nothing in my name. Ask, and you will receive, that your joy may be full.

WHAT WILL I DO TO OBEY GOD TODAY?

_____
_____
_____
_____
_____
_____
_____

AFRICA

FACT
Cameroon is twice the size of Oregon.

FEBRUARY 29

Read Mark 15:21–47 (older kids)
Read Mark 15:21–32 (younger kids)

TODAY'S PRAYER COUNTRY

CAMEROON

There are 14 million Muslim Fulani people here. Pray that they will come to Christ.

WHAT DID I LEARN FROM GOD'S WORD?

_____
_____
_____
_____

MONTHLY PRAYER PROMISE: John 16:24
Until now you have asked nothing in my name. Ask, and you will receive, that your joy may be full.

WHAT WILL I DO TO OBEY GOD TODAY?

_____
_____
_____
_____
_____
_____
_____

AFRICA

FACT
The official languages of Cameroon are French and English, and there are about twenty-four African dialects.

MARCH 1

Read Mark 16 (older kids)
Read Mark 16:14–20 (younger kids)

TODAY'S PRAYER COUNTRY
CANADA

Toronto claims to be the most racially diverse city in the world. Pray for good evangelism and discipleship in this city.

WHAT DID I LEARN FROM GOD'S WORD?

_____
_____
_____
_____

MONTHLY PRAYER PROMISE: Psalm 2:8
Ask of Me, and I will make the nations your heritage, and the ends of the earth your possession.

WHAT WILL I DO TO OBEY GOD TODAY?

_____
_____
_____
_____
_____
_____
_____

NORTH AMERICA

FACT
The St. Lawrence River and its tributaries are navigable for 1,900 miles.

MARCH 2

Read Luke 1:1–38 (older kids)
Read Luke 1:26–38 (younger kids)

TODAY'S PRAYER COUNTRY
CANADA

Many people in Canada are Catholic but never attend church. Pray for them.

WHAT DID I LEARN FROM GOD'S WORD?

_____

_____

_____

_____

MONTHLY PRAYER PROMISE: Psalm 2:8
Ask of Me, and I will make the nations your heritage, and the ends of the earth your possession.

WHAT WILL I DO TO OBEY GOD TODAY?

_____

_____

_____

_____

_____

_____

NORTH AMERICA

FACT
Canada is a country of ten provinces and three territories.

MARCH 3

Read Luke 1:39–80 (older kids)
Read Luke 1:46–55 (younger kids)

TODAY'S PRAYER COUNTRY

CENTRAL AFRICAN REPUBLIC (C.A.R.)

The number of Muslims in C.A.R. has been growing. Pray for more people to come to Christ.

WHAT DID I LEARN FROM GOD'S WORD?

_____
_____
_____
_____

MONTHLY PRAYER PROMISE: Psalm 2:8
Ask of Me, and I will make the nations your heritage, and the ends of the earth your possession.

WHAT WILL I DO TO OBEY GOD TODAY?

_____
_____
_____
_____
_____
_____
_____

AFRICA

FACT
There is only one AM radio station and one television broadcast station in C.A.R.

MARCH 4

Read Luke 2 (older kids)
Read Luke 2:1–7 (younger kids)

TODAY'S PRAYER COUNTRY

CENTRAL AFRICAN REPUBLIC (C.A.R.)

People here live (on average) only forty-three years and are in need of good medical care. Pray for medicine and care to reach them.

WHAT DID I LEARN FROM GOD'S WORD?

_____
_____
_____
_____

MONTHLY PRAYER PROMISE: Psalm 2:8
Ask of Me, and I will make the nations your heritage, and the ends of the earth your possession.

WHAT WILL I DO TO OBEY GOD TODAY?

_____
_____
_____
_____
_____
_____
_____

AFRICA

FACT
About half of the people in C.A.R. cannot read.

MARCH 5

Read Luke 3 (older kids)
Read Luke 3:1–6 (younger kids)

TODAY'S PRAYER COUNTRY

CHAD

Pray for the people of Chad. Most live in extreme poverty and cannot read.

WHAT DID I LEARN FROM GOD'S WORD?

MONTHLY PRAYER PROMISE: Psalm 2:8
Ask of Me, and I will make the nations your heritage, and the ends of the earth your possession.

WHAT WILL I DO TO OBEY GOD TODAY?

AFRICA

FACT
Chad has two official languages: French and Arabic.

MARCH 6

Read Luke 4:1–15 (older kids)
Read Luke 4:1–13 (younger kids)

TODAY'S PRAYER COUNTRY

CHAD

With 200 people groups and 120 languages in Chad, it is very hard to reach people with the gospel.

WHAT DID I LEARN FROM GOD'S WORD?

_____
_____
_____
_____

MONTHLY PRAYER PROMISE: Psalm 2:8
Ask of Me, and I will make the nations your heritage, and the ends of the earth your possession.

WHAT WILL I DO TO OBEY GOD TODAY?

_____
_____
_____
_____
_____
_____
_____

AFRICA

FACT
Oil revenues in Chad are estimated to earn $2.5 billion in the next thirty years.

MARCH 7

Read Luke 4:16–44 (older kids)
Read Luke 4:38–44 (younger kids)

TODAY'S PRAYER COUNTRY

CHILE

Drug abuse is a major problem in Chile. Pray the people will learn that true satisfaction comes from Jesus Christ.

WHAT DID I LEARN FROM GOD'S WORD?

_____

_____

_____

_____

MONTHLY PRAYER PROMISE: Psalm 2:8
Ask of Me, and I will make the nations your heritage, and the ends of the earth your possession.

WHAT WILL I DO TO OBEY GOD TODAY?

_____

_____

_____

_____

_____

_____

_____

SOUTH AMERICA

FACT
Chile won its independence from Spain in 1818.

MARCH 8

Read Luke 5 (older kids)
Read Luke 5:27–32 (younger kids)

TODAY'S PRAYER COUNTRY

CHILE

Chile is a deeply divided nation. Pray for them to find the Prince of Peace.

WHAT DID I LEARN FROM GOD'S WORD?

_____
_____
_____
_____

MONTHLY PRAYER PROMISE: Psalm 2:8
Ask of Me, and I will make the nations your heritage, and the ends of the earth your possession.

WHAT WILL I DO TO OBEY GOD TODAY?

_____
_____
_____
_____
_____
_____
_____

SOUTH AMERICA

FACT
About ninety percent of the people who live in Chile are Catholics.

MARCH 9

Read Luke 6:1–23 (older kids)
Read Luke 6:20–23 (younger kids)

TODAY'S PRAYER COUNTRY

CHINA

Pray for the 1.3 billion people in China. Most of them do not know who Jesus Christ really is.

WHAT DID I LEARN FROM GOD'S WORD?

_____
_____
_____
_____

MONTHLY PRAYER PROMISE: Psalm 2:8
Ask of Me, and I will make the nations your heritage, and the ends of the earth your possession.

WHAT WILL I DO TO OBEY GOD TODAY?

_____
_____
_____
_____
_____
_____
_____

ASIA

FACT
China has more people than any other country in the world.

MARCH 10

Read Luke 6:24–49 (older kids)
Read Luke 6:27–36 (younger kids)

TODAY'S PRAYER COUNTRY

CHINA

It is illegal to teach children about God in China. Pray for this to change.

WHAT DID I LEARN FROM GOD'S WORD?

_____
_____
_____
_____

MONTHLY PRAYER PROMISE: Psalm 2:8
Ask of Me, and I will make the nations your heritage, and the ends of the earth your possession.

WHAT WILL I DO TO OBEY GOD TODAY?

_____
_____
_____
_____
_____
_____
_____

FACT
One out of every five people in the world live in China.

MARGH 11

Read Luke 7:1–17 (older kids)
Read Luke 7:11–17 (younger kids)

TODAY'S PRAYER COUNTRY

COLOMBIA

Tens of thousands of children here have no home and live in the streets among the drug dealers. Pray for them.

WHAT DID I LEARN FROM GOD'S WORD?

_____
_____
_____
_____

MONTHLY PRAYER PROMISE: Psalm 2:8
Ask of Me, and I will make the nations your heritage, and the ends of the earth your possession.

WHAT WILL I DO TO OBEY GOD TODAY?

_____
_____
_____
_____
_____
_____
_____

SOUTH AMERICA

FACT
Colombia supplies seventy-five percent of the world's cocaine.

MARCH 12

Read Luke 7:18–50 (older kids)
Read Luke 7:41–50 (younger kids)

TODAY'S PRAYER COUNTRY

COLOMBIA

Pray for the Bellavista Prison in Medellin, Colombia, where many maximum security prisoners are hearing about Jesus Christ.

WHAT DID I LEARN FROM GOD'S WORD?

_____
_____
_____
_____

MONTHLY PRAYER PROMISE: Psalm 2:8
Ask of Me, and I will make the nations your heritage, and the ends of the earth your possession.

WHAT WILL I DO TO OBEY GOD TODAY?

_____
_____
_____
_____
_____
_____
_____

SOUTH AMERICA

FACT
Five billion dollars worth of illegal drugs come from Colombia to the US annually.

MARCH 13

Read Luke 8 (older kids)
Read Luke 8:9–15 (younger kids)

TODAY'S PRAYER COUNTRY
COMORO ISLANDS

Almost the entire population of these islands is Muslim. There are 780 Muslim mosques but no official churches.

WHAT DID I LEARN FROM GOD'S WORD?

_____
_____
_____
_____

MONTHLY PRAYER PROMISE: Psalm 2:8
Ask of Me, and I will make the nations your heritage, and the ends of the earth your possession.

WHAT WILL I DO TO OBEY GOD TODAY?

_____
_____
_____
_____
_____
_____
_____

AFRICA

FACT
The Comoro Islands are located off the east African coast in the Indian Ocean.

MARCH 14

Read Luke 9 (older kids)
Read Luke 9:57–62 (younger kids)

TODAY'S PRAYER COUNTRY

CONGO

Many families here are deeply affected by the AIDS virus. Pray for these families.

WHAT DID I LEARN FROM GOD'S WORD?

_____

_____

_____

_____

MONTHLY PRAYER PROMISE: Psalm 2:8
Ask of Me, and I will make the nations your heritage, and the ends of the earth your possession.

WHAT WILL I DO TO OBEY GOD TODAY?

_____

_____

_____

_____

_____

_____

_____

AFRICA

FACT
At least 90,000 people have died of AIDS in the Congo.

MARCH 15

Read Luke 10:1–24 (older kids)
Read Luke 10:1–12 (younger kids)

TODAY'S PRAYER COUNTRY

COSTA RICA

Pray for Bible-believing churches to be established among the tribes living in Costa Rica.

WHAT DID I LEARN FROM GOD'S WORD?

_____
_____
_____
_____

MONTHLY PRAYER PROMISE: Psalm 2:8
Ask of Me, and I will make the nations your heritage, and the ends of the earth your possession.

WHAT WILL I DO TO OBEY GOD TODAY?

_____
_____
_____
_____
_____
_____

NORTH AMERICA

FACT
One of every five people in Costa Rica live in deep poverty.

MARCH 16

Read Luke 10:25–42 (older kids)
Read Luke 10:25–37 (younger kids)

TODAY'S PRAYER COUNTRY

COSTA RICA

Costa Rican churches are missions-minded, and many missionaries are going out from this country. Pray for this to continue.

WHAT DID I LEARN FROM GOD'S WORD?

_____
_____
_____
_____

MONTHLY PRAYER PROMISE: Psalm 2:8
Ask of Me, and I will make the nations your heritage, and the ends of the earth your possession.

WHAT WILL I DO TO OBEY GOD TODAY?

_____
_____
_____
_____
_____
_____
_____

NORTH AMERICA

FACT
Columbus explored Costa Rica in 1502. The Spanish conquest began in 1524.

MARCH 17

Read Luke 11 (older kids)
Read Luke 11:1–13 (younger kids)

TODAY'S PRAYER COUNTRY
COTE D'IVOIRE

Pray for missionaries who are reaching out to Muslims in this French-speaking African country.

WHAT DID I LEARN FROM GOD'S WORD?

_____
_____
_____
_____

MONTHLY PRAYER PROMISE: Psalm 2:8
Ask of Me, and I will make the nations your heritage, and the ends of the earth your possession.

WHAT WILL I DO TO OBEY GOD TODAY?

_____
_____
_____
_____
_____
_____

AFRICA

FACT
Cote d'Ivoire, or Ivory Coast, is the world's largest producer of cocoa.

MARCH 18

Read Luke 12 (older kids)
Read Luke 12:22–34 (younger kids)

TODAY'S PRAYER COUNTRY

COTE D'IVOIRE

Worshipping idols rather than worshipping God is popular here. Pray for these people to worship the true God.

WHAT DID I LEARN FROM GOD'S WORD?

_____

_____

_____

_____

MONTHLY PRAYER PROMISE: Psalm 2:8
Ask of Me, and I will make the nations your heritage, and the ends of the earth your possession.

WHAT WILL I DO TO OBEY GOD TODAY?

_____

_____

_____

_____

_____

_____

_____

AFRICA

FACT
The number of people living in the cities of this country doubles every ten years.

MARCH 19

Read Luke 13:1–17 (older kids)
Read Luke 13:1–5 (younger kids)

TODAY'S PRAYER COUNTRY

CROATIA

There is deep hatred between the different peoples living in Croatia. Pray for the love of God to impact this country.

WHAT DID I LEARN FROM GOD'S WORD?

_____
_____
_____
_____

MONTHLY PRAYER PROMISE: Psalm 2:8
Ask of Me, and I will make the nations your heritage, and the ends of the earth your possession.

WHAT WILL I DO TO OBEY GOD TODAY?

_____
_____
_____
_____
_____
_____

EUROPE

FACT
There are forests in over one-third of Croatia.

MARGH 20

Read Luke 13:18–35 (older kids)
Read Luke 13:22–30 (younger kids)

TODAY'S PRAYER COUNTRY

GROATIA

Pray for Croatians to not only be religious (which they are) but also to come to know Christ.

WHAT DID I LEARN FROM GOD'S WORD?

_____
_____
_____
_____

MONTHLY PRAYER PROMISE: Psalm 2:8
Ask of Me, and I will make the nations your heritage, and the ends of the earth your possession.

WHAT WILL I DO TO OBEY GOD TODAY?

_____
_____
_____
_____
_____
_____
_____

EUROPE

FACT
Germany invaded this country in 1941. It was not until 1990 that free elections were held for the first time.

MARCH 21

Read Luke 14 (older kids)
Read Luke 14:25–35 (younger kids)

TODAY'S PRAYER COUNTRY

CUBA

For many years, Christians have been put in prison in Cuba. Pray for this to end.

WHAT DID I LEARN FROM GOD'S WORD?

_____
_____
_____
_____

MONTHLY PRAYER PROMISE: Psalm 2:8
Ask of Me, and I will make the nations your heritage, and the ends of the earth your possession.

WHAT WILL I DO TO OBEY GOD TODAY?

_____
_____
_____
_____
_____
_____
_____

NORTH AMERICA

FACT
Cuba is the largest of the Caribbean Islands.

MARCH 22

Read Luke 15 (older kids)
Read Luke 15:1–7 (younger kids)

TODAY'S PRAYER COUNTRY
CUBA

Many Cubans are members of a cult. Pray for these people to leave their false religion and come to Christ.

WHAT DID I LEARN FROM GOD'S WORD?

_____
_____
_____
_____

MONTHLY PRAYER PROMISE: Psalm 2:8
Ask of Me, and I will make the nations your heritage, and the ends of the earth your possession.

WHAT WILL I DO TO OBEY GOD TODAY?

_____
_____
_____
_____
_____
_____
_____

NORTH AMERICA

FACT
Cuba has the fewest tourists of all the Caribbean Islands.

MARCH 23

Read Luke 16:1–18 (older kids)
Read Luke 16:1–13 (younger kids)

TODAY'S PRAYER COUNTRY

CYPRUS

Pray for peace among all people living in this country.

WHAT DID I LEARN FROM GOD'S WORD?

MONTHLY PRAYER PROMISE: Psalm 2:8
Ask of Me, and I will make the nations your heritage, and the ends of the earth your possession.

WHAT WILL I DO TO OBEY GOD TODAY?

FACT
Cyprus is a nation divided. The south is known as the Republic of Cyprus.

MARCH 24

Read Luke 16:19–31 (older kids)
Read Luke 16:19–31 (younger kids)

TODAY'S PRAYER COUNTRY

CYPRUS

There are only a few Christians in the northern part of Cyprus because of the Muslim influence. Pray for more Christians in the north.

WHAT DID I LEARN FROM GOD'S WORD?

_____
_____
_____
_____

MONTHLY PRAYER PROMISE: Psalm 2:8
Ask of Me, and I will make the nations your heritage, and the ends of the earth your possession.

WHAT WILL I DO TO OBEY GOD TODAY?

_____
_____
_____
_____
_____
_____

ASIA

FACT
The northern part of Cyprus is known as the Turkish Republic of Northern Cyprus.

MARCH 25

Read Luke 17 (older kids)
Read Luke 17:1–6 (younger kids)

TODAY'S PRAYER COUNTRY
CZECH REPUBLIC

Many young people are searching for answers to life. Pray that Christians here would want to share their faith in Jesus Christ.

WHAT DID I LEARN FROM GOD'S WORD?

MONTHLY PRAYER PROMISE: Psalm 2:8
Ask of Me, and I will make the nations your heritage, and the ends of the earth your possession.

WHAT WILL I DO TO OBEY GOD TODAY?

EUROPE

FACT
The Czech Republic and Slovakia were united from November of 1918 until communism ended in 1992.

MARCH 26

Read Luke 18 (older kids)
Read Luke 18:1–8 (younger kids)

TODAY'S PRAYER COUNTRY

CZECH REPUBLIC

Because of drug abuse and crime, many families are finding it hard to stay together. Pray for these families.

WHAT DID I LEARN FROM GOD'S WORD?

_____

_____

_____

_____

MONTHLY PRAYER PROMISE: Psalm 2:8
Ask of Me, and I will make the nations your heritage, and the ends of the earth your possession.

WHAT WILL I DO TO OBEY GOD TODAY?

_____

_____

_____

_____

_____

_____

_____

EUROPE

FACT
Fifty percent of the people in this country describe themselves as atheists.

MARCH 27

Read Luke 19:1–27 (older kids)
Read Luke 19:1–10 (younger kids)

TODAY'S PRAYER COUNTRY

DENMARK

Many here are looking for something to fill the emptiness in their heart. Pray for revival in Denmark.

WHAT DID I LEARN FROM GOD'S WORD?

_____

_____

_____

_____

MONTHLY PRAYER PROMISE: Psalm 2:8
Ask of Me, and I will make the nations your heritage, and the ends of the earth your possession.

WHAT WILL I DO TO OBEY GOD TODAY?

_____

_____

_____

_____

_____

_____

_____

EUROPE

FACT
Denmark gives one percent of its national income to poor countries (ten times what the US gives).

MARCH 28

Read Luke 19:28–48 (older kids)
Read Luke 19:41–44 (younger kids)

TODAY'S PRAYER COUNTRY

DENMARK

Most people belong to a church but do not attend regularly. Pray for these people to attend Bible-believing churches.

WHAT DID I LEARN FROM GOD'S WORD?

_____

_____

_____

_____

MONTHLY PRAYER PROMISE: Psalm 2:8
Ask of Me, and I will make the nations your heritage, and the ends of the earth your possession.

WHAT WILL I DO TO OBEY GOD TODAY?

_____

_____

_____

_____

_____

_____

_____

EUROPE

FACT
The Danes invented Legos®, which means "I play" in Danish.

MARCH 29

Read Luke 20:1–26 (older kids)
Read Luke 20:9–18 (younger kids)

TODAY'S PRAYER COUNTRY
DJIBOUTI

Many Ethiopian refugees have escaped to Djibouti. Pray for them.

WHAT DID I LEARN FROM GOD'S WORD?

_____
_____
_____
_____

MONTHLY PRAYER PROMISE: Psalm 2:8
Ask of Me, and I will make the nations your heritage, and the ends of the earth your possession.

WHAT WILL I DO TO OBEY GOD TODAY?

_____
_____
_____
_____
_____
_____
_____

AFRICA

FACT
Djibouti is the third-smallest country on the continent of Africa.

MARCH 30

Read Luke 20:27–47 (older kids)
Read Luke 20:41–47 (younger kids)

TODAY'S PRAYER COUNTRY

DOMINICA

Pray for church leaders in Dominica because the country is quite poor and many church leaders have to work other jobs.

WHAT DID I LEARN FROM GOD'S WORD?

_____

_____

_____

_____

MONTHLY PRAYER PROMISE: Psalm 2:8
Ask of Me, and I will make the nations your heritage, and the ends of the earth your possession.

WHAT WILL I DO TO OBEY GOD TODAY?

_____

_____

_____

_____

_____

_____

_____

SOUTH AMERICA

FACT
Dominica, located in the Caribbean, was explored by Columbus in 1493.

MARCH 31

Read Luke 21 (older kids)
Read Luke 21:34–38 (younger kids)

TODAY'S PRAYER COUNTRY

DOMINICAN REPUBLIC

Pray that God's people will have willing hearts to serve as missionaries in the poor areas of this country.

WHAT DID I LEARN FROM GOD'S WORD?

MONTHLY PRAYER PROMISE: Psalm 2:8
Ask of Me, and I will make the nations your heritage, and the ends of the earth your possession.

WHAT WILL I DO TO OBEY GOD TODAY?

NORTH AMERICA

FACT
The Dominican Republic shares the island of Hispaniola with Haiti.

APRIL 1

Read Luke 22:1–38 (older kids)
Read Luke 22:24–30 (younger kids)

TODAY'S PRAYER COUNTRY

ECUADOR

Pray that people will reach out to the more than 1 million poor Ecuadorians who live in the slums here.

WHAT DID I LEARN FROM GOD'S WORD?

MONTHLY PRAYER PROMISE: Matthew 21:22
And whatever you ask in prayer, you will receive, if you have faith.

WHAT WILL I DO TO OBEY GOD TODAY?

SOUTH AMERICA

FACT
Ecuador ships more bananas around the world than any other country.

APRIL 2

Read Luke 22:39–71 (older kids)
Read Luke 22:39–46 (younger kids)

TODAY'S PRAYER COUNTRY

ECUADOR

Pray for peace and an honest government so that Ecuadorians can live to honor God.

WHAT DID I LEARN FROM GOD'S WORD?

MONTHLY PRAYER PROMISE: Matthew 21:22
And whatever you ask in prayer, you will receive, if you have faith.

WHAT WILL I DO TO OBEY GOD TODAY?

SOUTH AMERICA

FACT
Forty percent of the people who live in Ecuador are Quichua, native Amerindians.

APRIL 3

Read Luke 23 (older kids)
Read Luke 23:32–43 (younger kids)

TODAY'S PRAYER COUNTRY

EAST TIMOR

In East Timor, many young people and their parents have lost their homes. Pray for them as they live on the streets.

WHAT DID I LEARN FROM GOD'S WORD?

_____
_____
_____
_____

MONTHLY PRAYER PROMISE: Matthew 21:22
And whatever you ask in prayer, you will receive, if you have faith.

WHAT WILL I DO TO OBEY GOD TODAY?

_____
_____
_____
_____
_____
_____

AUSTRALASIA

FACT
Fifty percent of the people who live in East Timor do not have jobs.

APRIL 4

Read Luke 24 (older kids)
Read Luke 24:1–12 (younger kids)

TODAY'S PRAYER COUNTRY
EAST TIMOR

Twenty languages are spoken in East Timor. Pray for believers to reach out to all language groups in this country.

WHAT DID I LEARN FROM GOD'S WORD?

_____

_____

_____

_____

MONTHLY PRAYER PROMISE: Matthew 21:22
And whatever you ask in prayer, you will receive, if you have faith.

WHAT WILL I DO TO OBEY GOD TODAY?

_____

_____

_____

_____

_____

_____

_____

AUSTRALASIA

FACT
East Timor's closest neighbor is Australia, which is 400 miles to the south.

APRIL 5

Read John 1:1–28 (older kids)
Read John 1:29–34 (younger kids)

TODAY'S PRAYER COUNTRY

EGYPT

Persecution of Christians in Egypt is on the increase. Pray for the believers in Egypt to be free to worship God.

WHAT DID I LEARN FROM GOD'S WORD?

_____
_____
_____
_____

MONTHLY PRAYER PROMISE: Matthew 21:22
And whatever you ask in prayer, you will receive, if you have faith.

WHAT WILL I DO TO OBEY GOD TODAY?

_____
_____
_____
_____
_____
_____
_____

AFRICA

FACT
Ninety percent of the people who live in Egypt are Muslim.

APRIL 6

Read John 1:29–51 (older kids)
Read John 1:35–42 (younger kids)

TODAY'S PRAYER COUNTRY

EGYPT

Egyptian Christians could be valuable in reaching other Muslim countries in the Middle East with Christianity. Pray for them.

WHAT DID I LEARN FROM GOD'S WORD?

_____
_____
_____
_____

MONTHLY PRAYER PROMISE: Matthew 21:22
And whatever you ask in prayer, you will receive, if you have faith.

WHAT WILL I DO TO OBEY GOD TODAY?

_____
_____
_____
_____
_____
_____
_____

AFRICA

FACT
The Bible is available in all three languages used in Egypt.

APRIL 7

Read John 2 (older kids)
Read John 2:1–12 (younger kids)

TODAY'S PRAYER COUNTRY

EL SALVADOR

Twenty-two percent of the people here are now committed Christians; pray for them to spread the Good News of Jesus Christ.

WHAT DID I LEARN FROM GOD'S WORD?

_____
_____
_____
_____

MONTHLY PRAYER PROMISE: Matthew 21:22
And whatever you ask in prayer, you will receive, if you have faith.

WHAT WILL I DO TO OBEY GOD TODAY?

_____
_____
_____
_____
_____
_____
_____

NORTH AMERICA

FACT
El Salvador is the smallest of the Central American countries.

APRIL 8

Read John 3 (older kids)
Read John 3:16–21 (younger kids)

TODAY'S PRAYER COUNTRY
EL SALVADOR

Over 350,000 children were abandoned during a recent civil war and now live on the streets. Pray for these children.

WHAT DID I LEARN FROM GOD'S WORD?

MONTHLY PRAYER PROMISE: Matthew 21:22
And whatever you ask in prayer, you will receive, if you have faith.

WHAT WILL I DO TO OBEY GOD TODAY?

NORTH AMERICA

FACT
In March of 2006, El Salvador was the first Central American country to sign a free trade agreement with the US.

APRIL 9

Read John 4 (older kids)
Read John 4:46–54 (younger kids)

TODAY'S PRAYER COUNTRY
ENGLAND

The teenage suicide rate is very high in England. Pray for young people there to find hope in Jesus Christ.

WHAT DID I LEARN FROM GOD'S WORD?

MONTHLY PRAYER PROMISE: Matthew 21:22
And whatever you ask in prayer, you will receive, if you have faith.

WHAT WILL I DO TO OBEY GOD TODAY?

EUROPE

FACT
England has existed as a unified country since the tenth century.

APRIL 10

Read John 5 (older kids)
Read John 5:19–29 (younger kids)

TODAY'S PRAYER COUNTRY

ENGLAND

London is one of the world's most important cities. Pray for churches to reach out to the people in London.

WHAT DID I LEARN FROM GOD'S WORD?

_____
_____
_____
_____

MONTHLY PRAYER PROMISE: Matthew 21:22
And whatever you ask in prayer, you will receive, if you have faith.

WHAT WILL I DO TO OBEY GOD TODAY?

_____
_____
_____
_____
_____
_____
_____

EUROPE

FACT
Margaret Thatcher became England's first woman prime minister in 1979.

APRIL 11

Read John 6:1–21 (older kids)
Read John 6:16–21 (younger kids)

TODAY'S PRAYER COUNTRY

EQUATORIAL GUINEA

Pray for churches to have more freedom to share the gospel in this African country.

WHAT DID I LEARN FROM GOD'S WORD?

_____
_____
_____
_____

MONTHLY PRAYER PROMISE: Matthew 21:22
And whatever you ask in prayer, you will receive, if you have faith.

WHAT WILL I DO TO OBEY GOD TODAY?

_____
_____
_____
_____
_____
_____
_____

AFRICA

FACT
Equatorial Guinea became independent from Spain in 1978.

APRIL 12

Read John 6:22–71 (older kids)
Read John 6:60–71 (younger kids)

TODAY'S PRAYER COUNTRY
ERITREA

One-third of the people are Tigre, who are almost all Muslim. Pray for them.

WHAT DID I LEARN FROM GOD'S WORD?

_____
_____
_____
_____

MONTHLY PRAYER PROMISE: Matthew 21:22
And whatever you ask in prayer, you will receive, if you have faith.

WHAT WILL I DO TO OBEY GOD TODAY?

_____
_____
_____
_____
_____
_____
_____

AFRICA

FACT
Eritrea and Ethiopia fought the longest African civil war of the 20th century. Eritrea finally gained independence in 1993.

APRIL 13

Read John 7:1–24 (older kids)
Read John 7:1–9 (younger kids)

TODAY'S PRAYER COUNTRY

ESTONIA

Pray that God will cause the people of Estonia to seek Him.

WHAT DID I LEARN FROM GOD'S WORD?

_____
_____
_____
_____

MONTHLY PRAYER PROMISE: Matthew 21:22
And whatever you ask in prayer, you will receive, if you have faith.

WHAT WILL I DO TO OBEY GOD TODAY?

_____
_____
_____
_____
_____
_____
_____

EUROPE

FACT
Estonia is the northernmost country of the Baltic States and includes more than 1,500 islands.

APRIL 14

Read John 7:25–52 (older kids)
Read John 7:25–31 (younger kids)

TODAY'S PRAYER COUNTRY

ESTONIA

Praise God that people who live in Estonia can now worship God freely.

WHAT DID I LEARN FROM GOD'S WORD?

MONTHLY PRAYER PROMISE: Matthew 21:22
And whatever you ask in prayer, you will receive, if you have faith.

WHAT WILL I DO TO OBEY GOD TODAY?

EUROPE

FACT
The Estonian people and language are closely related to the people and language of Finland.

APRIL 15

Read John 8:1–30 (older kids)
Read John 8:12–18 (younger kids)

TODAY'S PRAYER COUNTRY

ETHIOPIA

Ethiopia is facing a real lack of food for its people. Pray for those who are starving.

WHAT DID I LEARN FROM GOD'S WORD?

MONTHLY PRAYER PROMISE: Matthew 21:22
And whatever you ask in prayer, you will receive, if you have faith.

WHAT WILL I DO TO OBEY GOD TODAY?

AFRICA

FACT
About 10 million Ethiopians are in desperate need of food.

APRIL 16

Read John 8:31–59 (older kids)
Read John 8:31–38 (younger kids)

TODAY'S PRAYER COUNTRY

ETHIOPIA

Ten percent of adult Ethiopians have AIDS. Pray for Christians to provide care and counseling for those who suffer.

WHAT DID I LEARN FROM GOD'S WORD?

_____

_____

_____

_____

MONTHLY PRAYER PROMISE: Matthew 21:22
And whatever you ask in prayer, you will receive, if you have faith.

WHAT WILL I DO TO OBEY GOD TODAY?

_____

_____

_____

_____

_____

_____

AFRICA

FACT
Ethiopians like to claim that they discovered coffee.

APRIL 17

Read John 9 (older kids)
Read John 9:35–41 (younger kids)

TODAY'S PRAYER COUNTRY

FIJI

Fiji is the largest non-Christian community in the Pacific. Pray for Fijians to come to Christ.

WHAT DID I LEARN FROM GOD'S WORD?

_____
_____
_____
_____

MONTHLY PRAYER PROMISE: Matthew 21:22
And whatever you ask in prayer, you will receive, if you have faith.

WHAT WILL I DO TO OBEY GOD TODAY?

_____
_____
_____
_____
_____
_____

AUSTRALASIA

FACT
Fiji is made up of two larger islands and 900 smaller mini-islands.

APRIL 18

Read John 10 (older kids)
Read John 10:7–18 (younger kids)

TODAY'S PRAYER COUNTRY
FIJI

Pray that there will be evangelistic churches started on the islands.

WHAT DID I LEARN FROM GOD'S WORD?

_____
_____
_____
_____

MONTHLY PRAYER PROMISE: Matthew 21:22
And whatever you ask in prayer, you will receive, if you have faith.

WHAT WILL I DO TO OBEY GOD TODAY?

_____
_____
_____
_____
_____
_____

AUSTRALASIA

FACT
People live on about 110 of the islands of Fiji.

APRIL 19

Read John 11:1–37 (older kids)
Read John 11:17–27 (younger kids)

TODAY'S PRAYER COUNTRY

FINLAND

Two out of every three Finns feel depressed about life and lack hope. Pray for them to see true hope in the Lord Jesus Christ.

WHAT DID I LEARN FROM GOD'S WORD?

_____
_____
_____
_____

MONTHLY PRAYER PROMISE: Matthew 21:22
And whatever you ask in prayer, you will receive, if you have faith.

WHAT WILL I DO TO OBEY GOD TODAY?

_____
_____
_____
_____
_____
_____
_____

EUROPE

FACT
Finland was ruled by Sweden for 700 years, until 1809.

APRIL 20

Read John 11:38–57 (older kids)
Read John 11:38–44 (younger kids)

TODAY'S PRAYER COUNTRY

FINLAND

There are lots of opportunities for Finnish Christians to share Christ; pray for them to be bold in sharing their faith.

WHAT DID I LEARN FROM GOD'S WORD?

_____
_____
_____
_____

MONTHLY PRAYER PROMISE: Matthew 21:22
And whatever you ask in prayer, you will receive, if you have faith.

WHAT WILL I DO TO OBEY GOD TODAY?

_____
_____
_____
_____
_____
_____
_____

EUROPE

FACT
Finns invented the sauna, and nearly every home has one.

APRIL 21

Read John 12:1–26 (older kids)
Read John 12:12–19 (younger kids)

TODAY'S PRAYER COUNTRY

FRANCE

The drop-out rate for missionaries is very high because many of them are discouraged. Pray for encouragement among those already there.

WHAT DID I LEARN FROM GOD'S WORD?

_____
_____
_____
_____

MONTHLY PRAYER PROMISE: Matthew 21:22
And whatever you ask in prayer, you will receive, if you have faith.

WHAT WILL I DO TO OBEY GOD TODAY?

_____
_____
_____
_____
_____
_____
_____

EUROPE

FACT
France is the largest country in Western Europe.

APRIL 22

Read John 12:27–50 (older kids)
Read John 12:44–50 (younger kids)

TODAY'S PRAYER COUNTRY

FRANCE

There are many French people who belong to cults. Pray for them to turn to Christ.

WHAT DID I LEARN FROM GOD'S WORD?

MONTHLY PRAYER PROMISE: Matthew 21:22
And whatever you ask in prayer, you will receive, if you have faith.

WHAT WILL I DO TO OBEY GOD TODAY?

EUROPE

FACT
Eighty percent of the French youth have never seen or held a Bible.

APRIL 23

Read John 13 (older kids)
Read John 13:31–35 (younger kids)

TODAY'S PRAYER COUNTRY

GABON

Pray that churches can be good witnesses to the growing number of Muslims in Gabon.

WHAT DID I LEARN FROM GOD'S WORD?

_____
_____
_____
_____

MONTHLY PRAYER PROMISE: Matthew 21:22
And whatever you ask in prayer, you will receive, if you have faith.

WHAT WILL I DO TO OBEY GOD TODAY?

_____
_____
_____
_____
_____
_____
_____

AFRICA

FACT
Most of Gabon is covered by dense tropical forest.

APRIL 24

Read John 14 (older kids)
Read John 14:1–6 (younger kids)

TODAY'S PRAYER COUNTRY

GAMBIA

Pray that Gambian Christians will be encouraged to help new converts grow.

WHAT DID I LEARN FROM GOD'S WORD?

_____
_____
_____
_____

MONTHLY PRAYER PROMISE: Matthew 21:22
And whatever you ask in prayer, you will receive, if you have faith.

WHAT WILL I DO TO OBEY GOD TODAY?

_____
_____
_____
_____
_____
_____
_____

FACT
Gambia, the smallest country on the continent of Africa, averages only twenty miles in width.

APRIL 25

Read John 15 (older kids)
Read John 15:1–11 (younger kids)

TODAY'S PRAYER COUNTRY

GEORGIA

Five people groups in Georgia do not have a Bible in their language. Pray for translators to help.

WHAT DID I LEARN FROM GOD'S WORD?

_____
_____
_____
_____

MONTHLY PRAYER PROMISE: Matthew 21:22
And whatever you ask in prayer, you will receive, if you have faith.

WHAT WILL I DO TO OBEY GOD TODAY?

_____
_____
_____
_____
_____
_____
_____

ASIA

FACT
Steel and aircraft are the main industrial products of Georgia.

APRIL 26

Read John 16 (older kids)
Read John 16:25–33 (younger kids)

TODAY'S PRAYER COUNTRY

GEORGIA

Pray for more Bible-believing churches in Georgia.

WHAT DID I LEARN FROM GOD'S WORD?

_____
_____
_____
_____

MONTHLY PRAYER PROMISE: Matthew 21:22
And whatever you ask in prayer, you will receive, if you have faith.

WHAT WILL I DO TO OBEY GOD TODAY?

_____
_____
_____
_____
_____
_____
_____

FACT
Georgia proclaimed its independence from Russia in 1991.

APRIL 27

Read John 17:1–19 (older kids)
Read John 17:1–5 (younger kids)

TODAY'S PRAYER COUNTRY

GERMANY

Most Germans would call themselves Christians, but only forty-five percent believe in God. Pray for them to turn to Christ.

WHAT DID I LEARN FROM GOD'S WORD?

_____
_____
_____
_____

MONTHLY PRAYER PROMISE: Matthew 21:22
And whatever you ask in prayer, you will receive, if you have faith.

WHAT WILL I DO TO OBEY GOD TODAY?

_____
_____
_____
_____
_____
_____

EUROPE

FACT
With over 82 million people, Germany is the most populated of the European Union member states.

APRIL 28

Read John 17:20–26 (older kids)
Read John 17:20–26 (younger kids)

TODAY'S PRAYER COUNTRY

GERMANY

The Church is considered unimportant by most Germans. Pray that they will learn how to worship the true God.

WHAT DID I LEARN FROM GOD'S WORD?

_____
_____
_____
_____

MONTHLY PRAYER PROMISE: Matthew 21:22
And whatever you ask in prayer, you will receive, if you have faith.

WHAT WILL I DO TO OBEY GOD TODAY?

_____
_____
_____
_____
_____
_____
_____

EUROPE

FACT
In 1727 Count Zinzendorf started a prayer meeting that lasted for 100 years, with individuals praying for one hour each.

APRIL 29

Read John 18:1–18 (older kids)
Read John 18:15–18 (younger kids)

TODAY'S PRAYER COUNTRY

GHANA

Seventy percent of the villages here have no church. Pray for good Bible-believing churches to be started.

WHAT DID I LEARN FROM GOD'S WORD?

_____
_____
_____
_____

MONTHLY PRAYER PROMISE: Matthew 21:22
And whatever you ask in prayer, you will receive, if you have faith.

WHAT WILL I DO TO OBEY GOD TODAY?

_____
_____
_____
_____
_____
_____
_____

AFRICA

FACT
In 1957, Ghana became the first British colony to gain independence.

APRIL 30

Read John 18:19–40 (older kids)
Read John 18:33–40 (younger kids)

TODAY'S PRAYER COUNTRY

GHANA

In Ghana, 45,000 children have been abandoned and are now homeless. Pray for these lonely children living on the streets.

WHAT DID I LEARN FROM GOD'S WORD?

_____
_____
_____
_____

MONTHLY PRAYER PROMISE: Matthew 21:22
And whatever you ask in prayer, you will receive, if you have faith.

WHAT WILL I DO TO OBEY GOD TODAY?

_____
_____
_____
_____
_____
_____
_____

AFRICA

FACT
Ghana is the second-largest producer of gold in Africa.

MAY 1

Read John 19 (older kids)
Read John 19:28–37 (younger kids)

TODAY'S PRAYER COUNTRY

GREAT BRITAIN

Christians in Great Britain used to reach people for Jesus Christ, but recently they have not done this very much. Pray for them to experience revival.

WHAT DID I LEARN FROM GOD'S WORD?

MONTHLY PRAYER PROMISE: Jeremiah 33:3
Call to me and I will answer you, and will tell you great and hidden things that you have not known.

WHAT WILL I DO TO OBEY GOD TODAY?

EUROPE

FACT
Great Britain was the world's first industrialized nation.

MAY 2

Read John 20 (older kids)
Read John 20:1–10 (younger kids)

TODAY'S PRAYER COUNTRY

GREAT BRITAIN

Pray for the large number of Bengalis who live in Great Britain. They need Christ.

WHAT DID I LEARN FROM GOD'S WORD?

_____

_____

_____

_____

MONTHLY PRAYER PROMISE: Jeremiah 33:3
Call to me and I will answer you, and will tell you great and hidden things that you have not known.

WHAT WILL I DO TO OBEY GOD TODAY?

_____

_____

_____

_____

_____

_____

_____

EUROPE

FACT
Great Britain includes these countries: England, Scotland, Wales, and Northern Ireland.

MAY 3

Read John 21:1–14 (older kids)
Read John 21:1–14 (younger kids)

TODAY'S PRAYER COUNTRY

GREECE

Pray that Greek Christians would have boldness to share their faith in God.

WHAT DID I LEARN FROM GOD'S WORD?

_____
_____
_____
_____

MONTHLY PRAYER PROMISE: Jeremiah 33:3
Call to me and I will answer you, and will tell you great and hidden things that you have not known.

WHAT WILL I DO TO OBEY GOD TODAY?

_____
_____
_____
_____
_____
_____
_____

EUROPE

FACT
The country of Greece includes more than 200 islands.

MAY 4

Read John 21:15–25 (older kids)
Read John 21:15–25 (younger kids)

TODAY'S PRAYER COUNTRY
GREECE

Although Greece is considered a Christian nation, pray that people will hear the gospel of Jesus Christ and respond.

WHAT DID I LEARN FROM GOD'S WORD?

_____
_____
_____
_____

MONTHLY PRAYER PROMISE: Jeremiah 33:3
Call to me and I will answer you, and will tell you great and hidden things that you have not known.

WHAT WILL I DO TO OBEY GOD TODAY?

_____
_____
_____
_____
_____
_____

FACT
Greece was the first European country to ever hear the gospel.

MAY 5

Read Acts 1 (older kids)
Read Acts 1:1–11 (younger kids)

TODAY'S PRAYER COUNTRY

GRENADA

Many people here would call themselves Christians but do not have a personal relationship with Jesus Christ.

WHAT DID I LEARN FROM GOD'S WORD?

_____
_____
_____
_____

MONTHLY PRAYER PROMISE: Jeremiah 33:3
Call to me and I will answer you, and will tell you great and hidden things that you have not known.

WHAT WILL I DO TO OBEY GOD TODAY?

_____
_____
_____
_____
_____
_____
_____

SOUTH AMERICA

FACT
In Grenada, the people are mostly of African descent and speak English.

MAY 6

Read Acts 2:1–13 (older kids)
Read Acts 2:5–13 (younger kids)

TODAY'S PRAYER COUNTRY

GUATEMALA

Pray for Guatemalans to turn themselves over to God completely.

WHAT DID I LEARN FROM GOD'S WORD?

_____
_____
_____
_____

MONTHLY PRAYER PROMISE: Jeremiah 33:3
Call to me and I will answer you, and will tell you great and hidden things that you have not known.

WHAT WILL I DO TO OBEY GOD TODAY?

_____
_____
_____
_____
_____
_____
_____

NORTH AMERICA

FACT
Ninety percent of the people in Guatemala live in poverty.

MAY 7

Read Acts 2:14–47 (older kids)
Read Acts 2:42–47 (younger kids)

TODAY'S PRAYER COUNTRY

GUATEMALA

Pray for the 5,000 children who live on the streets in Guatemala City, the capital of Guatemala.

WHAT DID I LEARN FROM GOD'S WORD?

_____
_____
_____
_____

MONTHLY PRAYER PROMISE: Jeremiah 33:3
Call to me and I will answer you, and will tell you great and hidden things that you have not known.

WHAT WILL I DO TO OBEY GOD TODAY?

_____
_____
_____
_____
_____
_____
_____

NORTH AMERICA

FACT
Guatemala is the largest country in Central America.

MAY 8

Read Acts 3 (older kids)
Read Acts 3:1–10 (younger kids)

TODAY'S PRAYER COUNTRY

GUINEA

Christians from Guinea's Kissi and Toma tribes are going as missionaries to work with other people groups. Pray for them as they take Christ to others.

WHAT DID I LEARN FROM GOD'S WORD?

MONTHLY PRAYER PROMISE: Jeremiah 33:3
Call to me and I will answer you, and will tell you great and hidden things that you have not known.

WHAT WILL I DO TO OBEY GOD TODAY?

AFRICA

FACT
Half of the people who live in Guinea are under sixteen years of age.

MAY 9

Read Acts 4:1–22 (older kids)
Read Acts 4:5–12 (younger kids)

TODAY'S PRAYER COUNTRY

GUINEA

Pray for people here who live in deep poverty and have very little food, clothing, or shelter.

WHAT DID I LEARN FROM GOD'S WORD?

_____
_____
_____
_____

MONTHLY PRAYER PROMISE: Jeremiah 33:3
Call to me and I will answer you, and will tell you great and hidden things that you have not known.

WHAT WILL I DO TO OBEY GOD TODAY?

_____
_____
_____
_____
_____
_____
_____

AFRICA

FACT
Guinea is the second-poorest nation in the world.

MAY 10

Read Acts 4:23–37 (older kids)
Read Acts 4:32–37 (younger kids)

TODAY'S PRAYER COUNTRY
GUINEA-BISSAU

Pray for the people to be able to hear God's Word, since many cannot read.

WHAT DID I LEARN FROM GOD'S WORD?

MONTHLY PRAYER PROMISE: Jeremiah 33:3
Call to me and I will answer you, and will tell you great and hidden things that you have not known.

WHAT WILL I DO TO OBEY GOD TODAY?

AFRICA

FACT
Three-quarters of the people in Guinea-Bissau cannot read.

MAY 11

Read Acts 5:1–16 (older kids)
Read Acts 5:1–11 (younger kids)

TODAY'S PRAYER COUNTRY

GUYANA

Many people here practice witchcraft. Pray for them to turn to Christ alone.

WHAT DID I LEARN FROM GOD'S WORD?

_____
_____
_____
_____

MONTHLY PRAYER PROMISE: Jeremiah 33:3
Call to me and I will answer you, and will tell you great and hidden things that you have not known.

WHAT WILL I DO TO OBEY GOD TODAY?

_____
_____
_____
_____
_____
_____

SOUTH AMERICA

FACT
Guyana was first a Dutch and then a British colony. It became independent in 1966.

MAY 12

Read Acts 5:17–42 (older kids)
Read Acts 5:17–26 (younger kids)

TODAY'S PRAYER COUNTRY

GUYANA

There is much racial tension in Guyana. Pray for these people to find the Prince of Peace, Jesus Christ.

WHAT DID I LEARN FROM GOD'S WORD?

_____
_____
_____
_____

MONTHLY PRAYER PROMISE: Jeremiah 33:3
Call to me and I will answer you, and will tell you great and hidden things that you have not known.

WHAT WILL I DO TO OBEY GOD TODAY?

_____
_____
_____
_____
_____
_____

SOUTH AMERICA

FACT
Guyana is about the size of Idaho. A tropical rain forest covers eighty percent of the land.

MAY 13

Read Acts 6 (older kids)
Read Acts 6:1–7 (younger kids)

TODAY'S PRAYER COUNTRY

HAITI

Pray for those who teach, train, and disciple people in Haiti, where many cannot even read.

WHAT DID I LEARN FROM GOD'S WORD?

_____
_____
_____
_____

MONTHLY PRAYER PROMISE: Jeremiah 33:3
Call to me and I will answer you, and will tell you great and hidden things that you have not known.

WHAT WILL I DO TO OBEY GOD TODAY?

_____
_____
_____
_____
_____
_____
_____

NORTH AMERICA

FACT
Haiti is the western third of the island of Hispaniola. The Dominican Republic makes up the other two-thirds of the island.

MAY 14

Read Acts 7:1–29 (older kids)
Read Acts 7:1–8 (younger kids)

TODAY'S PRAYER COUNTRY
HAITI

Pray for honest and godly leaders in Haiti who will address the very poor living conditions. Many Haitians do not even have running water.

WHAT DID I LEARN FROM GOD'S WORD?

_____
_____
_____
_____

MONTHLY PRAYER PROMISE: Jeremiah 33:3
Call to me and I will answer you, and will tell you great and hidden things that you have not known.

WHAT WILL I DO TO OBEY GOD TODAY?

_____
_____
_____
_____
_____
_____
_____

NORTH AMERICA

FACT
Haiti was explored by Christopher Columbus on December 6, 1492.

MAY 15

Read Acts 7:30–60 (older kids)
Read Acts 7:54–60 (younger kids)

TODAY'S PRAYER COUNTRY

HONDURAS

Families have been torn apart due to the damage caused by Hurricane Mitch. Pray for families to attend church together.

WHAT DID I LEARN FROM GOD'S WORD?

_____

_____

_____

_____

MONTHLY PRAYER PROMISE: Jeremiah 33:3
Call to me and I will answer you, and will tell you great and hidden things that you have not known.

WHAT WILL I DO TO OBEY GOD TODAY?

_____

_____

_____

_____

_____

_____

_____

NORTH AMERICA

FACT
In 1998, Hurricane Mitch devastated Honduras, doing $3 billion worth of damage.

MAY 16

Read Acts 8 (older kids)
Read Acts 8:34–40 (younger kids)

TODAY'S PRAYER COUNTRY
HONDURAS

Pray for the 8,000 homeless children who live on the streets in Tegucigalpa, the capital city of Honduras.

WHAT DID I LEARN FROM GOD'S WORD?

MONTHLY PRAYER PROMISE: Jeremiah 33:3
Call to me and I will answer you, and will tell you great and hidden things that you have not known.

WHAT WILL I DO TO OBEY GOD TODAY?

NORTH AMERICA

FACT
Honduras declared its independence from Spain in 1821.

MAY 17

Read Acts 9:1–19 (older kids)
Read Acts 9:1–9 (younger kids)

TODAY'S PRAYER COUNTRY

HUNGARY

Pray for the 200,000 refugees from Yugoslavia living in Hungary. They need Jesus Christ.

WHAT DID I LEARN FROM GOD'S WORD?

_____
_____
_____
_____

MONTHLY PRAYER PROMISE: Jeremiah 33:3
Call to me and I will answer you, and will tell you great and hidden things that you have not known.

WHAT WILL I DO TO OBEY GOD TODAY?

_____
_____
_____
_____
_____
_____
_____

EUROPE

FACT
Communist rule lasted in Hungary from 1945 to 1991.

MAY 18

Read Acts 9:20–43 (older kids)
Read Acts 9:32–43 (younger kids)

TODAY'S PRAYER COUNTRY

HUNGARY

Many young people here are open to hearing the gospel of Jesus Christ. Pray for Christians to talk to them.

WHAT DID I LEARN FROM GOD'S WORD?

_____

_____

_____

_____

MONTHLY PRAYER PROMISE: Jeremiah 33:3
Call to me and I will answer you, and will tell you great and hidden things that you have not known.

WHAT WILL I DO TO OBEY GOD TODAY?

_____

_____

_____

_____

_____

_____

EUROPE

FACT
The capital city, Budapest, is divided by the Danube River, with Buda on one side and Pest on the other.

MAY 19

Read Acts 10 (older kids)
Read Acts 10:1–8 (younger kids)

TODAY'S PRAYER COUNTRY
IGELAND

Iceland is a secular society drifting away from God. Pray for them to turn to God.

WHAT DID I LEARN FROM GOD'S WORD?

_____
_____
_____
_____

MONTHLY PRAYER PROMISE: Jeremiah 33:3
Call to me and I will answer you, and will tell you great and hidden things that you have not known.

WHAT WILL I DO TO OBEY GOD TODAY?

_____
_____
_____
_____
_____
_____
_____
_____

EUROPE

FACT
The Gulf Stream keeps the climate milder than one would expect for a country so near the Arctic.

MAY 20

Read Acts 11 (older kids)
Read Acts 11:19–30 (younger kids)

TODAY'S PRAYER COUNTRY

ICELAND

Pray for people here to build churches that are evangelistic and strong in their love for Jesus.

WHAT DID I LEARN FROM GOD'S WORD?

_____
_____
_____
_____

MONTHLY PRAYER PROMISE: Jeremiah 33:3
Call to me and I will answer you, and will tell you great and hidden things that you have not known.

WHAT WILL I DO TO OBEY GOD TODAY?

_____
_____
_____
_____
_____
_____
_____

EUROPE

FACT
More than thirteen percent of the land in Iceland is covered by snowfields and glaciers.

MAY 21

Read Acts 12 (older kids)
Read Acts 12:20–25 (younger kids)

TODAY'S PRAYER COUNTRY

INDIA

Pray for the 4 million orphans in India.

WHAT DID I LEARN FROM GOD'S WORD?

_____
_____
_____
_____

MONTHLY PRAYER PROMISE: Jeremiah 33:3
Call to me and I will answer you, and will tell you great and hidden things that you have not known.

WHAT WILL I DO TO OBEY GOD TODAY?

_____
_____
_____
_____
_____
_____
_____

ASIA

FACT
More than 1 billion people live in this country, which is one-third the size of the United States.

MAY 22

Read Acts 13:1–12 (older kids)
Read Acts 13:1–12 (younger kids)

TODAY'S PRAYER COUNTRY

INDIA

Pray for the many cities in India that have no gospel witness or church.

WHAT DID I LEARN FROM GOD'S WORD?

_____

_____

_____

_____

MONTHLY PRAYER PROMISE: Jeremiah 33:3
Call to me and I will answer you, and will tell you great and hidden things that you have not known.

WHAT WILL I DO TO OBEY GOD TODAY?

_____

_____

_____

_____

_____

_____

ASIA

FACT
Forty-one million people live in this country's city slums.

MAY 23

Read Acts 13:13–52 (older kids)
Read Acts 13:44–52 (younger kids)

TODAY'S PRAYER COUNTRY

INDONESIA

More Muslims live in Indonesia than any other country in the world. Pray for them to come to Jesus Christ.

WHAT DID I LEARN FROM GOD'S WORD?

MONTHLY PRAYER PROMISE: Jeremiah 33:3
Call to me and I will answer you, and will tell you great and hidden things that you have not known.

WHAT WILL I DO TO OBEY GOD TODAY?

AUSTRALASIA

FACT
Indonesia has 17,000 islands; people live on 6,000 of these islands.

MAY 24

Read Acts 14 (older kids)
Read Acts 14:1–7 (younger kids)

TODAY'S PRAYER COUNTRY

INDONESIA

Pray for Sumatra, the largest unevangelized island in the world.

WHAT DID I LEARN FROM GOD'S WORD?

_____
_____
_____
_____

MONTHLY PRAYER PROMISE: Jeremiah 33:3
Call to me and I will answer you, and will tell you great and hidden things that you have not known.

WHAT WILL I DO TO OBEY GOD TODAY?

_____
_____
_____
_____
_____
_____
_____

AUSTRALASIA

FACT
Indonesia has the largest number of active volcanoes of any country in the world.

MAY 25

Read Acts 15:1–21 (older kids)
Read Acts 15:1–11 (younger kids)

TODAY'S PRAYER COUNTRY

IRAN

There is no religious freedom in Iran. Pray for Christians who experience strong persecution.

WHAT DID I LEARN FROM GOD'S WORD?

_____
_____
_____
_____

MONTHLY PRAYER PROMISE: Jeremiah 33:3
Call to me and I will answer you, and will tell you great and hidden things that you have not known.

WHAT WILL I DO TO OBEY GOD TODAY?

_____
_____
_____
_____
_____
_____
_____

ASIA

FACT
Iran has been under Islamic government since 1979.

MAY 26

Read Acts 15:22–41 (older kids)
Read Acts 15:22–25 (younger kids)

TODAY'S PRAYER COUNTRY

IRAN

Pray for the gospel to go out to those who live in Iran. Millions of Iranians need Jesus Christ.

WHAT DID I LEARN FROM GOD'S WORD?

MONTHLY PRAYER PROMISE: Jeremiah 33:3
Call to me and I will answer you, and will tell you great and hidden things that you have not known.

WHAT WILL I DO TO OBEY GOD TODAY?

FACT
Ninety-eight percent of the people of Iran are Muslim.

MAY 27

Read Acts 16 (older kids)
Read Acts 16:25–34 (younger kids)

TODAY'S PRAYER COUNTRY

IRAQ

Pray for protection for believers living in Iraq.

WHAT DID I LEARN FROM GOD'S WORD?

_____
_____
_____
_____

MONTHLY PRAYER PROMISE: Jeremiah 33:3
Call to me and I will answer you, and will tell you great and hidden things that you have not known.

WHAT WILL I DO TO OBEY GOD TODAY?

_____
_____
_____
_____
_____
_____
_____

ASIA

FACT
Ninety-seven percent of the people who live in Iraq are Muslims.

MAY 28

Read Acts 17 (older kids)
Read Acts 17:1–9 (younger kids)

TODAY'S PRAYER COUNTRY

IRAQ

Pray that the Iraqi government will allow religious freedom.

WHAT DID I LEARN FROM GOD'S WORD?

MONTHLY PRAYER PROMISE: Jeremiah 33:3
Call to me and I will answer you, and will tell you great and hidden things that you have not known.

WHAT WILL I DO TO OBEY GOD TODAY?

ASIA

FACT
The government of Saddam Hussein ended on April 9, 2003, when US and British forces invaded Iraq.

MAY 29

Read Acts 18:1–17 (older kids)
Read Acts 18:1–8 (younger kids)

TODAY'S PRAYER COUNTRY
IRELAND

The Irish used to send missionaries all over the world. Pray for them to get back to sending missionaries.

WHAT DID I LEARN FROM GOD'S WORD?

MONTHLY PRAYER PROMISE: Jeremiah 33:3
Call to me and I will answer you, and will tell you great and hidden things that you have not known.

WHAT WILL I DO TO OBEY GOD TODAY?

EUROPE

FACT
Ireland occupies the entire island except for the six counties that make up Northern Ireland.

MAY 30

Read Acts 18:18–28 (older kids)
Read Acts 18:24–28 (younger kids)

TODAY'S PRAYER COUNTRY

IRELAND

The Catholic church is very strong in Ireland. Pray for these people to have a real relationship with Jesus Christ.

WHAT DID I LEARN FROM GOD'S WORD?

_____

_____

_____

_____

MONTHLY PRAYER PROMISE: Jeremiah 33:3
Call to me and I will answer you, and will tell you great and hidden things that you have not known.

WHAT WILL I DO TO OBEY GOD TODAY?

_____

_____

_____

_____

_____

_____

_____

EUROPE

FACT
For over 700 years Ireland was under British rule.

MAY 31

Read Acts 19 (older kids)
Read Acts 19:1–10 (younger kids)

TODAY'S PRAYER COUNTRY
ISRAEL

The number of people coming to Christ is growing. Pray for these new Christians to be discipled.

WHAT DID I LEARN FROM GOD'S WORD?

_____
_____
_____
_____

MONTHLY PRAYER PROMISE: Jeremiah 33:3
Call to me and I will answer you, and will tell you great and hidden things that you have not known.

WHAT WILL I DO TO OBEY GOD TODAY?

_____
_____
_____
_____
_____
_____
_____

ASIA

FACT
Israel is slightly larger than Massachusetts.

JUNE 1

Read Acts 20 (older kids)
Read Acts 20:17–28 (younger kids)

TODAY'S PRAYER COUNTRY

ISRAEL

Pray that the power of God's grace and love would break through all religion and pride.

WHAT DID I LEARN FROM GOD'S WORD?

MONTHLY PRAYER PROMISE: Matthew 7:7
Ask, and it will be given to you; seek, and you will find; knock, and it will be opened to you.

WHAT WILL I DO TO OBEY GOD TODAY?

ASIA

FACT
Two percent of Israelis are Arab Christians.

JUNE 2

Read Acts 21 (older kids)
Read Acts 21: 27–36 (younger kids)

TODAY'S PRAYER COUNTRY
ITALY

There are 100,000 magicians here who follow the occult and Satanism. Pray for people to turn to Christ.

WHAT DID I LEARN FROM GOD'S WORD?

_____
_____
_____
_____

MONTHLY PRAYER PROMISE: Matthew 7:7
Ask, and it will be given to you; seek, and you will find; knock, and it will be opened to you.

WHAT WILL I DO TO OBEY GOD TODAY?

_____
_____
_____
_____
_____
_____

EUROPE

FACT
The country of Italy includes the islands of Sicily and Sardinia.

JUNE 3

Read Acts 22:1–21 (older kids)
Read Acts 22:1–11 (younger kids)

TODAY'S PRAYER COUNTRY
ITALY

There are not many Bible-preaching churches in the northern cities of Milan, Bologna, Turin, and Venice. Pray for new churches to be started.

WHAT DID I LEARN FROM GOD'S WORD?

_____

_____

_____

_____

MONTHLY PRAYER PROMISE: Matthew 7:7
Ask, and it will be given to you; seek, and you will find; knock, and it will be opened to you.

WHAT WILL I DO TO OBEY GOD TODAY?

_____

_____

_____

_____

_____

_____

_____

FACT
Vatican City, an enclave in Rome, is the location of the worldwide Catholic church headquarters.

JUNE 4

Read Acts 22:22–30 (older kids)
Read Acts 22:22–30 (younger kids)

TODAY'S PRAYER COUNTRY

JAMAICA

Violence, crime, and drugs are hurting many Jamaicans. Pray for Jamaicans to come to Christ.

WHAT DID I LEARN FROM GOD'S WORD?

MONTHLY PRAYER PROMISE: Matthew 7:7
Ask, and it will be given to you; seek, and you will find; knock, and it will be opened to you.

WHAT WILL I DO TO OBEY GOD TODAY?

NORTH AMERICA

FACT
Jamaica was explored by Columbus in 1494 and is the third-largest island in the Caribbean.

JUNE 5

Read Acts 23 (older kids)
Read Acts 23:23–35 (younger kids)

TODAY'S PRAYER COUNTRY
JAMAICA

Pray for students studying the Bible in Jamaica that God would use them as fresh leadership for churches there.

WHAT DID I LEARN FROM GOD'S WORD?

_____
_____
_____
_____

MONTHLY PRAYER PROMISE: Matthew 7:7
Ask, and it will be given to you; seek, and you will find; knock, and it will be opened to you.

WHAT WILL I DO TO OBEY GOD TODAY?

_____
_____
_____
_____
_____
_____
_____

NORTH AMERICA

FACT
Jamaica was ruled first by the Spanish, then by the British.

JUNE 6

Read Acts 24 (older kids)
Read Acts 24:10–21 (younger kids)

TODAY'S PRAYER COUNTRY

JAPAN

Most of the people here are into Shintoism, a religion that worships spirits and dead relatives. Pray for them to come to Christ.

WHAT DID I LEARN FROM GOD'S WORD?

_____

_____

_____

_____

MONTHLY PRAYER PROMISE: Matthew 7:7
Ask, and it will be given to you; seek, and you will find; knock, and it will be opened to you.

WHAT WILL I DO TO OBEY GOD TODAY?

_____

_____

_____

_____

_____

_____

ASIA

FACT
Half of the world's working robots are made in Japan. One model can even fetch your newspaper.

JUNE 7

TODAY'S PRAYER COUNTRY

JAPAN

Pray that Christians would present Christ boldly to those who attend Christian weddings.

WHAT DID I LEARN FROM GOD'S WORD?

MONTHLY PRAYER PROMISE: Matthew 7:7
Ask, and it will be given to you; seek, and you will find; knock, and it will be opened to you.

WHAT WILL I DO TO OBEY GOD TODAY?

ASIA

FACT
One-third of Japanese want to have Christian-style weddings.

JUNE 8

Read Acts 25:13–27 (older kids)
Read Acts 25:23–37 (younger kids)

TODAY'S PRAYER COUNTRY

JORDAN

Pray for people who are interested in knowing more about Jesus to turn to Him as their Lord and Savior.

WHAT DID I LEARN FROM GOD'S WORD?

MONTHLY PRAYER PROMISE: Matthew 7:7
Ask, and it will be given to you; seek, and you will find; knock, and it will be opened to you.

WHAT WILL I DO TO OBEY GOD TODAY?

ASIA

FACT
Thirty-five percent of the people in Jordan are interested in learning more about Jesus.

JUNE 9

Read Acts 26 (older kids)
Read Acts 26:12–18 (younger kids)

TODAY'S PRAYER COUNTRY

JORDAN

Over half the people in Jordan are under fifteen. Pray for the children and youth in Jordan to come to Christ.

WHAT DID I LEARN FROM GOD'S WORD?

_____
_____
_____
_____

MONTHLY PRAYER PROMISE: Matthew 7:7
Ask, and it will be given to you; seek, and you will find; knock, and it will be opened to you.

WHAT WILL I DO TO OBEY GOD TODAY?

_____
_____
_____
_____
_____
_____
_____

ASIA

FACT
In 1923, after the fall of the Ottoman Empire, Jordan was placed under British rule. In 1946, in reward for Jordan's loyalty during WWII, Great Britain granted Jordan independence.

JUNE 10

Read Acts 27:1–12 (older kids)
Read Acts 27:1–8 (younger kids)

TODAY'S PRAYER COUNTRY

KAZAKHSTAN

More Islamic missionaries are coming to Kazakhstan recently. Pray for more Christian missionaries to come to this country.

WHAT DID I LEARN FROM GOD'S WORD?

_____

_____

_____

_____

MONTHLY PRAYER PROMISE: Matthew 7:7
Ask, and it will be given to you; seek, and you will find; knock, and it will be opened to you.

WHAT WILL I DO TO OBEY GOD TODAY?

_____

_____

_____

_____

_____

_____

ASIA

FACT
Kazakhstan is the ninth-largest country in the world.

JUNE 11

Read Acts 27:13–44 (older kids)
Read Acts 27:39–44 (younger kids)

TODAY'S PRAYER COUNTRY
KAZAKHSTAN

Pray for the 40 million people whose health is affected by previous nuclear testing.

WHAT DID I LEARN FROM GOD'S WORD?

_____
_____
_____
_____

MONTHLY PRAYER PROMISE: Matthew 7:7
Ask, and it will be given to you; seek, and you will find; knock, and it will be opened to you.

WHAT WILL I DO TO OBEY GOD TODAY?

_____
_____
_____
_____
_____
_____
_____

ASIA

FACT
Since the 1940s, the Soviets have conducted massive nuclear testing in Kazakhstan.

JUNE 12

Read Acts 28 (older kids)
Read Acts 28:17–30 (younger kids)

TODAY'S PRAYER COUNTRY

KENYA

Pray for university students who believe in Jesus Christ to reach out to other students.

WHAT DID I LEARN FROM GOD'S WORD?

_____
_____
_____
_____

MONTHLY PRAYER PROMISE: Matthew 7:7
Ask, and it will be given to you; seek, and you will find; knock, and it will be opened to you.

WHAT WILL I DO TO OBEY GOD TODAY?

_____
_____
_____
_____
_____
_____
_____

AFRICA

FACT
Ten percent of the university students in Kenya are active Christians.

JUNE 13

Read Romans 1:1–15 (older kids)
Read Romans 1:8–15 (younger kids)

TODAY'S PRAYER COUNTRY
KENYA

There is more spiritual freedom in Kenya than there used to be. Pray for God to use this openness for His glory.

WHAT DID I LEARN FROM GOD'S WORD?

MONTHLY PRAYER PROMISE: Matthew 7:7
Ask, and it will be given to you; seek, and you will find; knock, and it will be opened to you.

WHAT WILL I DO TO OBEY GOD TODAY?

AFRICA

FACT
Fourteen percent of the adult population of Kenya are infected by the AIDS virus.

JUNE 14

Read Romans 1:16–32 (older kids)
Read Romans 1:16–25 (younger kids)

TODAY'S PRAYER COUNTRY

KIRIBATI

Pray that there would be active Christian witnesses on every island in Kiribati.

WHAT DID I LEARN FROM GOD'S WORD?

MONTHLY PRAYER PROMISE: Matthew 7:7
Ask, and it will be given to you; seek, and you will find; knock, and it will be opened to you.

WHAT WILL I DO TO OBEY GOD TODAY?

AUSTRALASIA

FACT
Kiribati consists of thirty-three tiny coral islands in the Pacific Ocean.

JUNE 15

Read Romans 2 (older kids)
Read Romans 2:1–11 (younger kids)

TODAY'S PRAYER COUNTRY
KOREA, NORTH

Pray for those who are persecuted here. Many are killed because of their faith in Jesus Christ.

WHAT DID I LEARN FROM GOD'S WORD?

MONTHLY PRAYER PROMISE: Matthew 7:7
Ask, and it will be given to you; seek, and you will find; knock, and it will be opened to you.

WHAT WILL I DO TO OBEY GOD TODAY?

ASIA

FACT
In North Korea, 100,000 Christians are being held in prison.

JUNE 16

Read Romans 3 (older kids)
Read Romans 3:9–20 (younger kids)

TODAY'S PRAYER COUNTRY

KOREA, NORTH

Millions are dying of starvation in North Korea. Pray that food will reach those who need it most.

WHAT DID I LEARN FROM GOD'S WORD?

MONTHLY PRAYER PROMISE: Matthew 7:7
Ask, and it will be given to you; seek, and you will find; knock, and it will be opened to you.

WHAT WILL I DO TO OBEY GOD TODAY?

ASIA

FACT
The New York Philharmonic played a concert in North Korea for the first time in February 2008.

JUNE 17

Read Romans 4:1–12 (older kids)
Read Romans 4:4–8 (younger kids)

TODAY'S PRAYER COUNTRY

KOREA, SOUTH

Pray that the Korean church will continue to be on fire for God.

WHAT DID I LEARN FROM GOD'S WORD?

MONTHLY PRAYER PROMISE: Matthew 7:7
Ask, and it will be given to you; seek, and you will find; knock, and it will be opened to you.

WHAT WILL I DO TO OBEY GOD TODAY?

ASIA

FACT
The ten largest churches in the world are in South Korea.

JUNE 18

Read Romans 4:13–25 (older kids)
Read Romans 4:19–25 (younger kids)

TODAY'S PRAYER COUNTRY

KOREA, SOUTH

Pray for the many churches in South Korea that are in need of pastors.

WHAT DID I LEARN FROM GOD'S WORD?

_____

_____

_____

_____

MONTHLY PRAYER PROMISE: Matthew 7:7
Ask, and it will be given to you; seek, and you will find; knock, and it will be opened to you.

WHAT WILL I DO TO OBEY GOD TODAY?

_____

_____

_____

_____

_____

_____

_____

ASIA

FACT
The South Korean economy is the eleventh largest in the world.

JUNE 19

Read Romans 5 (older kids)
Read Romans 5:12–21 (younger kids)

TODAY'S PRAYER COUNTRY

KUWAIT

There are only a few hundred Christians in Kuwait. Pray for more people in Kuwait to come to Christ.

WHAT DID I LEARN FROM GOD'S WORD?

_____

_____

_____

_____

MONTHLY PRAYER PROMISE: Matthew 7:7
Ask, and it will be given to you; seek, and you will find; knock, and it will be opened to you.

WHAT WILL I DO TO OBEY GOD TODAY?

_____

_____

_____

_____

_____

_____

_____

FACT
Kuwait is slightly larger than Hawaii.

JUNE 20

Read Romans 6:1–14 (older kids)
Read Romans 6:1–4 (younger kids)

TODAY'S PRAYER COUNTRY

KUWAIT

Many Muslims in Kuwait know very little about Jesus Christ. Pray for God to open doors in this country.

WHAT DID I LEARN FROM GOD'S WORD?

_____
_____
_____
_____

MONTHLY PRAYER PROMISE: Matthew 7:7
Ask, and it will be given to you; seek, and you will find; knock, and it will be opened to you.

WHAT WILL I DO TO OBEY GOD TODAY?

_____
_____
_____
_____
_____
_____
_____

ASIA

FACT
In April 2006, women in Kuwait were allowed to vote for the first time.

JUNE 21

Read Romans 6:15–23 (older kids)
Read Romans 6:20–23 (younger kids)

TODAY'S PRAYER COUNTRY

KYRGYZSTAN

Kyrgyzstan is a Muslim country, but very few people here know much about Islam. Pray for more openness to the gospel.

WHAT DID I LEARN FROM GOD'S WORD?

_____

_____

_____

_____

MONTHLY PRAYER PROMISE: Matthew 7:7
Ask, and it will be given to you; seek, and you will find; knock, and it will be opened to you.

WHAT WILL I DO TO OBEY GOD TODAY?

_____

_____

_____

_____

_____

_____

ASIA

FACT
Kyrgyzstan is the smallest and poorest of the Central Asian republics.

JUNE 22

Read Romans 7 (older kids)
Read Romans 7:1–6 (younger kids)

TODAY'S PRAYER COUNTRY

KYRGYZSTAN

Pray for new churches to be started in Kyrgyzstan.

WHAT DID I LEARN FROM GOD'S WORD?

_____
_____
_____
_____

MONTHLY PRAYER PROMISE: Matthew 7:7
Ask, and it will be given to you; seek, and you will find; knock, and it will be opened to you.

WHAT WILL I DO TO OBEY GOD TODAY?

_____
_____
_____
_____
_____
_____
_____

ASIA

FACT
About ninety percent of the people here live in poverty.

JUNE 23

Read Romans 8:1–17 (older kids)
Read Romans 8:1–11 (younger kids)

TODAY'S PRAYER COUNTRY

LAOS

It is dangerous and difficult for church leaders to get training. Pray for these pastors and church leaders.

WHAT DID I LEARN FROM GOD'S WORD?

_____
_____
_____
_____

MONTHLY PRAYER PROMISE: Matthew 7:7
Ask, and it will be given to you; seek, and you will find; knock, and it will be opened to you.

WHAT WILL I DO TO OBEY GOD TODAY?

_____
_____
_____
_____
_____
_____

ASIA

FACT
Laos gained independence from France in 1953.

JUNE 24

Read Romans 8:18–39 (older kids)
Read Romans 8:35–39 (younger kids)

TODAY'S PRAYER COUNTRY

LAOS

Despite much persecution of Christians, there are reports that whole villages are coming to Christ. Pray for these villages.

WHAT DID I LEARN FROM GOD'S WORD?

_____
_____
_____
_____

MONTHLY PRAYER PROMISE: Matthew 7:7
Ask, and it will be given to you; seek, and you will find; knock, and it will be opened to you.

WHAT WILL I DO TO OBEY GOD TODAY?

_____
_____
_____
_____
_____
_____

ASIA

FACT
Laos was heavily bombed by the United States during the Vietnam War.

JUNE 25

Read Romans 9 (older kids)
Read Romans 9:1–5 (younger kids)

TODAY'S PRAYER COUNTRY

LATVIA

Eighty percent of Latvian young people believe in God but have never begun a real relationship with Jesus Christ; pray for them.

WHAT DID I LEARN FROM GOD'S WORD?

_____
_____
_____
_____

MONTHLY PRAYER PROMISE: Matthew 7:7
Ask, and it will be given to you; seek, and you will find; knock, and it will be opened to you.

WHAT WILL I DO TO OBEY GOD TODAY?

_____
_____
_____
_____
_____
_____

EUROPE

FACT
Since the Middle Ages, Latvia has been ruled by Denmark, Russia, Germany, and Sweden.

JUNE 26

Read Romans 10 (older kids)
Read Romans 10:1–4 (younger kids)

TODAY'S PRAYER COUNTRY

LATVIA

Pray that Latvian church leaders can be trained, equipped, and supported to become better pastors.

WHAT DID I LEARN FROM GOD'S WORD?

_____
_____
_____
_____

MONTHLY PRAYER PROMISE: Matthew 7:7
Ask, and it will be given to you; seek, and you will find; knock, and it will be opened to you.

WHAT WILL I DO TO OBEY GOD TODAY?

_____
_____
_____
_____
_____
_____
_____

EUROPE

FACT
Latvia gained its independence from the Soviet Union in September 1991.

JUNE 27

Read Romans 11 (older kids)
Read Romans 11:33–36 (younger kids)

TODAY'S PRAYER COUNTRY

LEBANON

Pray for people who have seen so much war and terror to open their hearts to the Prince of Peace.

WHAT DID I LEARN FROM GOD'S WORD?

_____

_____

_____

_____

MONTHLY PRAYER PROMISE: Matthew 7:7
Ask, and it will be given to you; seek, and you will find; knock, and it will be opened to you.

WHAT WILL I DO TO OBEY GOD TODAY?

_____

_____

_____

_____

_____

_____

_____

ASIA

FACT
Lebanon is the only country in the Middle East that does not have a desert.

JUNE 28

Read Romans 12:1–8 (older kids)
Read Romans 12:1–2 (younger kids)

TODAY'S PRAYER COUNTRY

LEBANON

Pray for believers who are working in schools and orphanages. Pray that they would have a bold witness for Jesus.

WHAT DID I LEARN FROM GOD'S WORD?

_____
_____
_____
_____

MONTHLY PRAYER PROMISE: Matthew 7:7
Ask, and it will be given to you; seek, and you will find; knock, and it will be opened to you.

WHAT WILL I DO TO OBEY GOD TODAY?

_____
_____
_____
_____
_____
_____
_____

ASIA

FACT
Lebanon is the only Arab state that is not officially Muslim.

JUNE 29

Read Romans 12:9–21 (older kids)
Read Romans 12:9–13 (younger kids)

TODAY'S PRAYER COUNTRY

LESOTHO

Six hundred thousand people live in the mountains here and have no contact with Christians. Pray for missionaries to reach them.

WHAT DID I LEARN FROM GOD'S WORD?

_____
_____
_____
_____

MONTHLY PRAYER PROMISE: Matthew 7:7
Ask, and it will be given to you; seek, and you will find; knock, and it will be opened to you.

WHAT WILL I DO TO OBEY GOD TODAY?

_____
_____
_____
_____
_____
_____
_____

AFRICA

FACT
Lesotho is a mountainous country that is totally surrounded by the country of South Africa.

JUNE 30

Read Romans 13 (older kids)
Read Romans 13:1–7 (younger kids)

TODAY'S PRAYER COUNTRY

LESOTHO

Churches in Lesotho need money, leadership, vision, and people. Pray for them.

WHAT DID I LEARN FROM GOD'S WORD?

MONTHLY PRAYER PROMISE: Matthew 7:7
Ask, and it will be given to you; seek, and you will find; knock, and it will be opened to you.

WHAT WILL I DO TO OBEY GOD TODAY?

AFRICA

FACT
About twenty-five percent of the adults in Lesotho have AIDS.

JULY 1

Read Romans 14:1–12 (older kids)
Read Romans 14:10–12 (younger kids)

TODAY'S PRAYER COUNTRY
LIBERIA

Many missionaries were forced to leave Liberia because of a civil war. Pray that many more missionaries will return.

WHAT DID I LEARN FROM GOD'S WORD?

_____
_____
_____
_____

MONTHLY PRAYER PROMISE: Psalm 42:8
By day the LORD commands his steadfast love, and at night his song is with me, a prayer to the God of my life.

WHAT WILL I DO TO OBEY GOD TODAY?

_____
_____
_____
_____
_____
_____
_____

AFRICA

FACT
Liberia has an average yearly rainfall of 160 inches.

JULY 2

Read Romans 14:13–23 (older kids)
Read Romans 14:13–19 (younger kids)

TODAY'S PRAYER COUNTRY

LIBERIA

Pray for different ethnic groups in Liberia that hate each other. Pray that they will learn to love the way God loves.

WHAT DID I LEARN FROM GOD'S WORD?

_____
_____
_____
_____

MONTHLY PRAYER PROMISE: Psalm 42:8
By day the LORD commands his steadfast love, and at night his song is with me, a prayer to the God of my life.

WHAT WILL I DO TO OBEY GOD TODAY?

_____
_____
_____
_____
_____
_____
_____

AFRICA

FACT
Liberia was Africa's first republic. It was founded in 1822 to settle freed American slaves.

JULY 3

Read Romans 15:1–13 (older kids)
Read Romans 15:1–7 (younger kids)

TODAY'S PRAYER COUNTRY

LIBYA

Pray for God to open doors for the gospel to be proclaimed in Libya.

WHAT DID I LEARN FROM GOD'S WORD?

_____

_____

_____

_____

MONTHLY PRAYER PROMISE: Psalm 42:8
By day the LORD commands his steadfast love, and at night his song is with me, a prayer to the God of my life.

WHAT WILL I DO TO OBEY GOD TODAY?

_____

_____

_____

_____

_____

_____

_____

AFRICA

FACT
Libya was transformed by the discovery of oil in 1959. For a long time, the wealth from this oil was used to spread international terrorism.

JULY 4

Read Romans 15:14–33 (older kids)
Read Romans 15:30–33 (younger kids)

TODAY'S PRAYER COUNTRY

LIBYA

There is no Bible in Libyan Arabic.
Pray for translators.

WHAT DID I LEARN FROM GOD'S WORD?

_____
_____
_____
_____

MONTHLY PRAYER PROMISE: Psalm 42:8
By day the LORD commands his steadfast love, and at night his song is with me, a prayer to
the God of my life.

WHAT WILL I DO TO OBEY GOD TODAY?

_____
_____
_____
_____
_____
_____
_____

AFRICA

FACT
The United States "Marine Hymn"
mentions "the shores of Tripoli,"
a location in Libya.

JULY 5

Read Romans 16 (older kids)
Read Romans 16:25–27 (younger kids)

TODAY'S PRAYER COUNTRY

LIECHTENSTEIN

Many people here are Catholics and have never made a personal commitment to Jesus Christ. Pray for them.

WHAT DID I LEARN FROM GOD'S WORD?

MONTHLY PRAYER PROMISE: Psalm 42:8
By day the LORD commands his steadfast love, and at night his song is with me, a prayer to the God of my life.

WHAT WILL I DO TO OBEY GOD TODAY?

EUROPE

FACT
The entire country of Liechtenstein is slightly smaller than Washington, D.C.

JULY 6

Read I Corinthians 1 (older kids)
Read 1 Corinthians 1:18–25 (younger kids)

TODAY'S PRAYER COUNTRY
LITHUANIA

Pray that Lithuania will be more open to the gospel and that more people will be willing to present it there.

WHAT DID I LEARN FROM GOD'S WORD?

MONTHLY PRAYER PROMISE: Psalm 42:8
By day the LORD commands his steadfast love, and at night his song is with me, a prayer to the God of my life.

WHAT WILL I DO TO OBEY GOD TODAY?

EUROPE

FACT
In 1991, Lithuania declared its independence from the Soviet Union.

JULY 7

Read 1 Corinthians 2:1–5 (older kids)
Read 1 Corinthians 2:1–5 (younger kids)

TODAY'S PRAYER COUNTRY

LITHUANIA

Pray that church leaders will be grounded in the Bible and not be led away by false teaching.

WHAT DID I LEARN FROM GOD'S WORD?

MONTHLY PRAYER PROMISE: Psalm 42:8
By day the LORD commands his steadfast love, and at night his song is with me, a prayer to the God of my life.

WHAT WILL I DO TO OBEY GOD TODAY?

EUROPE

FACT
Lithuania is a country of rolling hills and many forests, rivers, streams, and lakes.

JULY 8

Read 1 Corinthians 2:6–16 (older kids)
Read 1 Corinthians 2:9–13 (younger kids)

TODAY'S PRAYER COUNTRY

LUXEMBOURG

The Bible has not been translated into Letzebuergesch, which is the first language people here learn to speak.

WHAT DID I LEARN FROM GOD'S WORD?

_____

_____

_____

_____

MONTHLY PRAYER PROMISE: Psalm 42:8
By day the LORD commands his steadfast love, and at night his song is with me, a prayer to the God of my life.

WHAT WILL I DO TO OBEY GOD TODAY?

_____

_____

_____

_____

_____

_____

_____

EUROPE

FACT
Luxembourg became an independent state in 963 A.D.

JULY 9

Read 1 Corinthians 3 (older kids)
Read 1 Corinthians 3:1–9 (younger kids)

TODAY'S PRAYER COUNTRY

MACEDONIA

Pray that the small number of evangelical churches here will grow in their desire to see people saved.

WHAT DID I LEARN FROM GOD'S WORD?

_____
_____
_____
_____

MONTHLY PRAYER PROMISE: Psalm 42:8
By day the LORD commands his steadfast love, and at night his song is with me, a prayer to the God of my life.

WHAT WILL I DO TO OBEY GOD TODAY?

_____
_____
_____
_____
_____
_____
_____

FACT
A former republic of Yugoslavia, Macedonia became independent in 1991.

JULY 10

Read 1 Corinthians 4:1–7 (older kids)
Read 1 Corinthians 4:6–7 (younger kids)

TODAY'S PRAYER COUNTRY

MACEDONIA

The capital, Skopje, has the largest Roma (Gypsy) population in the world. Pray for churches to reach out to this people group.

WHAT DID I LEARN FROM GOD'S WORD?

_____
_____
_____
_____

MONTHLY PRAYER PROMISE: Psalm 42:8
By day the LORD commands his steadfast love, and at night his song is with me, a prayer to the God of my life.

WHAT WILL I DO TO OBEY GOD TODAY?

_____
_____
_____
_____
_____
_____
_____

EUROPE

FACT
The Kosovo crisis in 1999 caused many Albanians to flee to Macedonia.

JULY 11

Read 1 Corinthians 4:8–21 (older kids)
Read 1 Corinthians 4:14–21 (younger kids)

TODAY'S PRAYER COUNTRY

MADAGASCAR

Pray for all the people in remote villages to hear a gospel witness.

WHAT DID I LEARN FROM GOD'S WORD?

MONTHLY PRAYER PROMISE: Psalm 42:8
By day the LORD commands his steadfast love, and at night his song is with me, a prayer to the God of my life.

WHAT WILL I DO TO OBEY GOD TODAY?

AFRICA

FACT
Five million people live in remote villages in Madagascar.

JULY 12

Read 1 Corinthians 5 (older kids)
Read 1 Corinthians 5:9–13 (younger kids)

TODAY'S PRAYER COUNTRY

MADAGASCAR

Pray for missionaries who travel to the villages, often on their bicycles.

WHAT DID I LEARN FROM GOD'S WORD?

_____
_____
_____
_____

MONTHLY PRAYER PROMISE: Psalm 42:8
By day the LORD commands his steadfast love, and at night his song is with me, a prayer to the God of my life.

WHAT WILL I DO TO OBEY GOD TODAY?

_____
_____
_____
_____
_____
_____
_____

AFRICA

FACT
Madagascar is the world's fourth-largest island.

JULY 13

Read 1 Corinthians 6:1–11 (older kids)
Read 1 Corinthians 6:9–11 (younger kids)

TODAY'S PRAYER COUNTRY

MALAWI

Pray for Christians to share the gospel with the growing number of Muslims in Malawi.

WHAT DID I LEARN FROM GOD'S WORD?

_____
_____
_____
_____

MONTHLY PRAYER PROMISE: Psalm 42:8
By day the LORD commands his steadfast love, and at night his song is with me, a prayer to the God of my life.

WHAT WILL I DO TO OBEY GOD TODAY?

_____
_____
_____
_____
_____
_____
_____

AFRICA

FACT
Under a recent dictator, 250,000 people in Malawi died or disappeared.

JULY 14

Read 1 Corinthians 6:12–20 (older kids)
Read 1 Corinthians 6:19–20 (younger kids)

TODAY'S PRAYER COUNTRY

MALAYSIA

Because of Islamic influences, it is really difficult for believers in Christ to be discipled. Pray for these believers.

WHAT DID I LEARN FROM GOD'S WORD?

_____

_____

_____

_____

MONTHLY PRAYER PROMISE: Psalm 42:8
By day the LORD commands his steadfast love, and at night his song is with me, a prayer to the God of my life.

WHAT WILL I DO TO OBEY GOD TODAY?

_____

_____

_____

_____

_____

_____

_____

AUSTRALASIA

FACT
Malaysia's Petronas Twin Towers, at 1,482 feet, were the tallest buildings in the world from 1998 to 2004.

JULY 15

Read 1 Corinthians 7 (older kids)
Read 1 Corinthians 7:17–24 (younger kids)

TODAY'S PRAYER COUNTRY
MALAYSIA

Pray for the tribal groups in East Malaysia to hear about Jesus.

WHAT DID I LEARN FROM GOD'S WORD?

_____
_____
_____
_____

MONTHLY PRAYER PROMISE: Psalm 42:8
By day the LORD commands his steadfast love, and at night his song is with me, a prayer to the God of my life.

WHAT WILL I DO TO OBEY GOD TODAY?

_____
_____
_____
_____
_____
_____
_____

AUSTRALASIA

FACT
At one time, Michael Jordan made more money from Nike than all the Nike factory workers in Malaysia combined.

JULY 16

Read 1 Corinthians 8 (older kids)
Read 1 Corinthians 8:7–13 (younger kids)

TODAY'S PRAYER COUNTRY

MALDIVES

No Christian missionaries have ever been allowed into the Maldives. Pray for that to change.

WHAT DID I LEARN FROM GOD'S WORD?

_____
_____
_____
_____

MONTHLY PRAYER PROMISE: Psalm 42:8
By day the LORD commands his steadfast love, and at night his song is with me, a prayer to the God of my life.

WHAT WILL I DO TO OBEY GOD TODAY?

_____
_____
_____
_____
_____
_____
_____

Maldives is made up of 1,200 coral islands off the southwest coast of India.

JULY 17

Read 1 Corinthians 9 (older kids)
Read 1 Corinthians 9:24–27 (younger kids)

TODAY'S PRAYER COUNTRY
MALI

Pray for missionaries as they work with the largest ethnic group in Mali, the Bambara.

WHAT DID I LEARN FROM GOD'S WORD?

_____
_____
_____
_____

MONTHLY PRAYER PROMISE: Psalm 42:8
By day the LORD commands his steadfast love, and at night his song is with me, a prayer to the God of my life.

WHAT WILL I DO TO OBEY GOD TODAY?

_____
_____
_____
_____
_____
_____
_____

FACT
This African country is almost as big as Alaska.

JULY 18

Read 1 Corinthians 10:1–22 (older kids)
Read 1 Corinthians 10:1–5 (younger kids)

TODAY'S PRAYER COUNTRY

MALI

Pray for the northern part of Mali, which is mostly Muslim; these people need Jesus Christ.

WHAT DID I LEARN FROM GOD'S WORD?

_____
_____
_____
_____

MONTHLY PRAYER PROMISE: Psalm 42:8
By day the LORD commands his steadfast love, and at night his song is with me, a prayer to the God of my life.

WHAT WILL I DO TO OBEY GOD TODAY?

_____
_____
_____
_____
_____
_____
_____

AFRICA

FACT
Less than half of the people in Mali can read.

JULY 19

Read 1 Corinthians 10:23–33 (older kids)
Read 1 Corinthians 10:31–33 (younger kids)

TODAY'S PRAYER COUNTRY

MALTA

Pray that passion for evangelism will grow and that the Maltese will stand strong for what they believe.

WHAT DID I LEARN FROM GOD'S WORD?

_____
_____
_____
_____

MONTHLY PRAYER PROMISE: Psalm 42:8
By day the LORD commands his steadfast love, and at night his song is with me, a prayer to the God of my life.

WHAT WILL I DO TO OBEY GOD TODAY?

_____
_____
_____
_____
_____
_____
_____

FACT
There are five Maltese islands: Malta, Gozo, Comino, Cominotto, and Filfla.

JULY 20

Read 1 Corinthians 11:1–16 (older kids)
Read 1 Corinthians 11:1–7 (younger kids)

TODAY'S PRAYER COUNTRY

MALTA

Many Christians here face pressure because they follow Jesus Christ. Pray for them to be faithful witnesses.

WHAT DID I LEARN FROM GOD'S WORD?

MONTHLY PRAYER PROMISE: Psalm 42:8
By day the LORD commands his steadfast love, and at night his song is with me, a prayer to the God of my life.

WHAT WILL I DO TO OBEY GOD TODAY?

EUROPE

FACT
The five Maltese islands have a combined land area smaller than Philadelphia.

JULY 21

Read 1 Corinthians 11:17–34 (older kids)
Read 1 Corinthians 11:27–32 (younger kids)

TODAY'S PRAYER COUNTRY

MARSHALL ISLANDS

Pray for new spiritual life on these islands.

WHAT DID I LEARN FROM GOD'S WORD?

_____
_____
_____
_____

MONTHLY PRAYER PROMISE: Psalm 42:8
By day the LORD commands his steadfast love, and at night his song is with me, a prayer to the God of my life.

WHAT WILL I DO TO OBEY GOD TODAY?

_____
_____
_____
_____
_____
_____
_____

AUSTRALASIA

FACT
The Marshall Islands make up an area slightly larger than Washington, D.C.

JULY 22

Read 1 Corinthians 12 (older kids)
Read 1 Corinthians 12:1–11 (younger kids)

TODAY'S PRAYER COUNTRY

MAURITANIA

Obstacles to the gospel here include having no Bible in their language, being unable to read, and living in an Islamic culture.

WHAT DID I LEARN FROM GOD'S WORD?

_____
_____
_____
_____

MONTHLY PRAYER PROMISE: Psalm 42:8
By day the LORD commands his steadfast love, and at night his song is with me, a prayer to the God of my life.

WHAT WILL I DO TO OBEY GOD TODAY?

_____
_____
_____
_____
_____
_____
_____

FACT
Because of the desert, only one percent of the land is fertile enough to farm in this African country.

JULY 23

Read 1 Corinthians 13 (older kids)
Read 1 Corinthians 13:4–7 (younger kids)

TODAY'S PRAYER COUNTRY

MAURITIUS

There is much religious confusion.
Pray for the Holy Spirit to show that
Jesus Christ is the way, the truth,
and the life.

WHAT DID I LEARN FROM GOD'S WORD?

_____
_____
_____
_____

MONTHLY PRAYER PROMISE: Psalm 42:8
By day the LORD commands his steadfast love, and at night his song is with me, a prayer to
the God of my life.

WHAT WILL I DO TO OBEY GOD TODAY?

_____
_____
_____
_____
_____
_____
_____

AFRICA

FACT
Religions in Mauritius include
Hindu (48%), Catholic (24%),
and Muslim (17%).

JULY 24

Read 1 Corinthians 14:1–25 (older kids)
Read 1 Corinthians 14:20–25 (younger kids)

TODAY'S PRAYER COUNTRY

MAURITIUS

Pray for more missionaries to come to this African country.

WHAT DID I LEARN FROM GOD'S WORD?

MONTHLY PRAYER PROMISE: Psalm 42:8
By day the LORD commands his steadfast love, and at night his song is with me, a prayer to the God of my life.

WHAT WILL I DO TO OBEY GOD TODAY?

AFRICA

FACT
Mauritius is a mountainous island in the Indian Ocean east of Madagascar.

JULY 25

Read 1 Corinthians 15:1–34 (older kids)
Read 1 Corinthians 15:1–4 (younger kids)

TODAY'S PRAYER COUNTRY

MEXICO

Pray for the millions of students in Mexico who need to hear about Jesus Christ.

WHAT DID I LEARN FROM GOD'S WORD?

_____
_____
_____
_____

MONTHLY PRAYER PROMISE: Psalm 42:8
By day the LORD commands his steadfast love, and at night his song is with me, a prayer to the God of my life.

WHAT WILL I DO TO OBEY GOD TODAY?

_____
_____
_____
_____
_____
_____
_____

NORTH AMERICA

FACT
Each night, 600,000 children sleep on the streets here.

JULY 26

Read 1 Corinthians 15:35–58 (older kids)
Read 1 Corinthians 15:51–58 (younger kids)

TODAY'S PRAYER COUNTRY
MEXICO

Mexico City is one of the most polluted cities in the world. Pray for the gospel to reach the people of this great city.

WHAT DID I LEARN FROM GOD'S WORD?

_____
_____
_____
_____

MONTHLY PRAYER PROMISE: Psalm 42:8
By day the LORD commands his steadfast love, and at night his song is with me, a prayer to the God of my life.

WHAT WILL I DO TO OBEY GOD TODAY?

_____
_____
_____
_____
_____
_____
_____

NORTH AMERICA

FACT
Mexico City is the second-largest city in the world; only Tokyo, Japan, is larger.

JULY 27

Read 1 Corinthians 16 (older kids)
Read 1 Corinthians 16:1–4 (younger kids)

TODAY'S PRAYER COUNTRY

MICRONESIA

Magic is widely used on these islands. Pray for people to turn to Christ instead of magic.

WHAT DID I LEARN FROM GOD'S WORD?

_____

_____

_____

_____

MONTHLY PRAYER PROMISE: Psalm 42:8
By day the LORD commands his steadfast love, and at night his song is with me, a prayer to the God of my life.

WHAT WILL I DO TO OBEY GOD TODAY?

_____

_____

_____

_____

_____

_____

_____

AUSTRALASIA

FACT
Micronesia has about 2,000 islands; people live on about one hundred of these islands.

JULY 28

Read 2 Corinthians 1:1–11 (older kids)
Read 2 Corinthians 1:8–11 (younger kids)

TODAY'S PRAYER COUNTRY

MICRONESIA

One million Japanese tourists visit shrines here every year. Pray for churches to reach out to these tourists.

WHAT DID I LEARN FROM GOD'S WORD?

_____
_____
_____
_____

MONTHLY PRAYER PROMISE: Psalm 42:8
By day the LORD commands his steadfast love, and at night his song is with me, a prayer to the God of my life.

WHAT WILL I DO TO OBEY GOD TODAY?

_____
_____
_____
_____
_____
_____
_____

AUSTRALASIA

FACT
The Marshall Islands, North Marianas, and Palau are part of Micronesia.

JULY 29

TODAY'S PRAYER COUNTRY

MOLDOVA

Pray that people here who have a serious problem with alcohol will find that Jesus Christ will meet their needs.

WHAT DID I LEARN FROM GOD'S WORD?

_____
_____
_____
_____

MONTHLY PRAYER PROMISE: Psalm 42:8
By day the LORD commands his steadfast love, and at night his song is with me, a prayer to the God of my life.

WHAT WILL I DO TO OBEY GOD TODAY?

_____
_____
_____
_____
_____
_____
_____

EUROPE

FACT
Sixty percent of the people who live in Moldova have a serious alcohol problem.

JULY 30

Read 2 Corinthians 2:12–17 (older kids)
Read 2 Corinthians 2:14–17 (younger kids)

TODAY'S PRAYER COUNTRY

MOLDOVA

Moldova is a country still ruled by communists. Pray for these leaders to turn to the Lord Jesus.

WHAT DID I LEARN FROM GOD'S WORD?

_____
_____
_____
_____

MONTHLY PRAYER PROMISE: Psalm 42:8
By day the LORD commands his steadfast love, and at night his song is with me, a prayer to the God of my life.

WHAT WILL I DO TO OBEY GOD TODAY?

_____
_____
_____
_____
_____
_____

EUROPE

FACT
Moldova is the poorest country in Europe; eighty percent of the men are unemployed.

JULY 31

Read 2 Corinthians 3 (older kids)
Read 2 Corinthians 3:12–18 (younger kids)

TODAY'S PRAYER COUNTRY

MONACO

Pray for the three churches that serve this tiny country.

WHAT DID I LEARN FROM GOD'S WORD?

_____
_____
_____
_____

MONTHLY PRAYER PROMISE: Psalm 42:8
By day the LORD commands his steadfast love, and at night his song is with me, a prayer to the God of my life.

WHAT WILL I DO TO OBEY GOD TODAY?

_____
_____
_____
_____
_____
_____
_____

EUROPE

FACT
Monaco is the second-smallest country in the world, after Nauru, which is the smallest.

AUGUST 1

Read 2 Corinthians 4:1–6 (older kids)
Read 2 Corinthians 4:1–2 (younger kids)

TODAY'S PRAYER COUNTRY

MONGOLIA

Buddhism has a strong hold in Mongolia. Pray for these people to see that Jesus is the way, the truth, and the life.

WHAT DID I LEARN FROM GOD'S WORD?

_____

_____

_____

_____

MONTHLY PRAYER PROMISE: James 5:16
Therefore, confess your sins to one another and pray for one another, that you may be healed. The prayer of a righteous person has great power as it is working.

WHAT WILL I DO TO OBEY GOD TODAY?

_____

_____

_____

_____

_____

_____

_____

ASIA

FACT
One of Mongolia's most famous leaders was Genghis Khan, who lived in the thirteenth century.

AUGUST 2

Read 2 Corinthians 4:7–18 (older kids)
Read 2 Corinthians 4:16–18 (younger kids)

TODAY'S PRAYER COUNTRY

MONGOLIA

Pray for families to teach their children about Jesus and reach the next generation for Christ.

WHAT DID I LEARN FROM GOD'S WORD?

_____
_____
_____
_____

MONTHLY PRAYER PROMISE: James 5:16
Therefore, confess your sins to one another and pray for one another, that you may be healed. The prayer of a righteous person has great power as it is working.

WHAT WILL I DO TO OBEY GOD TODAY?

_____
_____
_____
_____
_____
_____
_____

ASIA

FACT
Forty percent of the people live a nomadic lifestyle, moving frequently with their houses and animals.

AUGUST 3

Read 2 Corinthians 5:1–10 (older kids)
Read 2 Corinthians 5:6–10 (younger kids)

TODAY'S PRAYER COUNTRY

MONTENEGRO

There is much religious hatred in Montenegro. Pray for Christians to be good examples of love and forgiveness.

WHAT DID I LEARN FROM GOD'S WORD?

_____
_____
_____
_____

MONTHLY PRAYER PROMISE: James 5:16
Therefore, confess your sins to one another and pray for one another, that you may be healed. The prayer of a righteous person has great power as it is working.

WHAT WILL I DO TO OBEY GOD TODAY?

_____
_____
_____
_____
_____
_____
_____

EUROPE

FACT
Montenegro, formerly Serbia and Montenegro, gained its independence in 2006.

AUGUST 4

Read 2 Corinthians 5:11–21 (older kids)
Read 2 Corinthians 5:16–21 (younger kids)

TODAY'S PRAYER COUNTRY

MONTENEGRO

Pray for peace in this country that has experienced so much war. Pray that the people here will find the Prince of Peace.

WHAT DID I LEARN FROM GOD'S WORD?

MONTHLY PRAYER PROMISE: James 5:16
Therefore, confess your sins to one another and pray for one another, that you may be healed. The prayer of a righteous person has great power as it is working.

WHAT WILL I DO TO OBEY GOD TODAY?

EUROPE

FACT
Montenegro was part of the old Yugoslavia, which was under communist rule for forty-five years.

AUGUST 5

Read 2 Corinthians 6:1–13 (older kids)
Read 2 Corinthians 6:11–13 (younger kids)

TODAY'S PRAYER COUNTRY

MOROCCO

Pray for the many people here with no job and no money to buy food or to meet daily needs.

WHAT DID I LEARN FROM GOD'S WORD?

MONTHLY PRAYER PROMISE: James 5:16
Therefore, confess your sins to one another and pray for one another, that you may be healed. The prayer of a righteous person has great power as it is working.

WHAT WILL I DO TO OBEY GOD TODAY?

AFRICA

FACT
Morocco is located on the northwest tip of Africa but is only eight miles from mainland Europe.

AUGUST 6

Read 2 Corinthians 6:14–18 (older kids)
Read 2 Corinthians 6:16–18 (younger kids)

TODAY'S PRAYER COUNTRY

MOROCCO

Pray that there will be greater freedom for Christians to share their faith and also for protection for those who get saved.

WHAT DID I LEARN FROM GOD'S WORD?

_____
_____
_____
_____

MONTHLY PRAYER PROMISE: James 5:16
Therefore, confess your sins to one another and pray for one another, that you may be healed. The prayer of a righteous person has great power as it is working.

WHAT WILL I DO TO OBEY GOD TODAY?

_____
_____
_____
_____
_____
_____
_____

AFRICA

FACT
The largest city in Morocco is Casablanca, with over 3 million people.

AUGUST 7

Read 2 Corinthians 7 (older kids)
Read 2 Corinthians 7:1–4 (younger kids)

TODAY'S PRAYER COUNTRY

MOZAMBIQUE

Over 300,000 children here have lost their parents to AIDS. Pray for these orphans.

WHAT DID I LEARN FROM GOD'S WORD?

MONTHLY PRAYER PROMISE: James 5:16
Therefore, confess your sins to one another and pray for one another, that you may be healed. The prayer of a righteous person has great power as it is working.

WHAT WILL I DO TO OBEY GOD TODAY?

AFRICA

FACT
Mozambique has twenty-five large rivers that flow into the Indian Ocean.

AUGUST 8

Read 2 Corinthians 8 (older kids)
Read 2 Corinthians 8:16–18 (younger kids)

TODAY'S PRAYER COUNTRY

MOZAMBIQUE

Many churches here lack good Bible teaching. Pray that more will become available.

WHAT DID I LEARN FROM GOD'S WORD?

_____
_____
_____
_____

MONTHLY PRAYER PROMISE: James 5:16
Therefore, confess your sins to one another and pray for one another, that you may be healed. The prayer of a righteous person has great power as it is working.

WHAT WILL I DO TO OBEY GOD TODAY?

_____
_____
_____
_____
_____
_____
_____

AFRICA

FACT
Mozambique was explored by Vasco da Gama in 1498 and colonized by Portugal in 1505.

AUGUST 9

Read 2 Corinthians 9 (older kids)
Read 2 Corinthians 9:6–9 (younger kids)

TODAY'S PRAYER COUNTRY

MYANMAR

The ruling military regime has tried to do away with all Christians. Pray for the military to come to Christ.

WHAT DID I LEARN FROM GOD'S WORD?

_____
_____
_____
_____

MONTHLY PRAYER PROMISE: James 5:16
Therefore, confess your sins to one another and pray for one another, that you may be healed. The prayer of a righteous person has great power as it is working.

WHAT WILL I DO TO OBEY GOD TODAY?

_____
_____
_____
_____
_____
_____
_____

ASIA

FACT
Mongolians under Kublai Khan invaded this country in the thirteenth century.

AUGUST 10

Read 2 Corinthians 10 (older kids)
Read 2 Corinthians 10:13–18 (younger kids)

TODAY'S PRAYER COUNTRY

MYANMAR

Pray that Christians will stay faithful to God as they face heavy persecution.

WHAT DID I LEARN FROM GOD'S WORD?

_____
_____
_____
_____

MONTHLY PRAYER PROMISE: James 5:16
Therefore, confess your sins to one another and pray for one another, that you may be healed. The prayer of a righteous person has great power as it is working.

WHAT WILL I DO TO OBEY GOD TODAY?

_____
_____
_____
_____
_____
_____
_____

ASIA

FACT
In 1886, Myanmar (formerly Burma) joined India; it became a separate colony in 1937.

AUGUST 11

Read 2 Corinthians 11:1–15 (older kids)
Read 2 Corinthians 11:1–6 (younger kids)

TODAY'S PRAYER COUNTRY
NAMIBIA

Many churches mix Christian beliefs with other beliefs such as the occult. Pray for them to follow Christ alone.

WHAT DID I LEARN FROM GOD'S WORD?

_____
_____
_____
_____

MONTHLY PRAYER PROMISE: James 5:16
Therefore, confess your sins to one another and pray for one another, that you may be healed. The prayer of a righteous person has great power as it is working.

WHAT WILL I DO TO OBEY GOD TODAY?

_____
_____
_____
_____
_____
_____
_____

AFRICA

FACT
After World War I, South Africa was given this German colony to "look after."

AUGUST 12

Read 2 Corinthians 11:16–33 (older kids)
Read 2 Corinthians 11:24–30 (younger kids)

TODAY'S PRAYER COUNTRY

NAURU

Pray for people who live in Nauru. This country is very rich and many people do not think they need Jesus Christ.

WHAT DID I LEARN FROM GOD'S WORD?

MONTHLY PRAYER PROMISE: James 5:16
Therefore, confess your sins to one another and pray for one another, that you may be healed. The prayer of a righteous person has great power as it is working.

WHAT WILL I DO TO OBEY GOD TODAY?

AUSTRALASIA

FACT
Located in the Pacific, Nauru is the world's smallest country.

AUGUST 13

Read 2 Corinthians 12:1–10 (older kids)
Read 2 Corinthians 12:9–10 (younger kids)

TODAY'S PRAYER COUNTRY
NEPAL

Before 1960, no Christian could even live in Nepal. Now there is more religious freedom. Pray that this continues.

WHAT DID I LEARN FROM GOD'S WORD?

_____
_____
_____
_____

MONTHLY PRAYER PROMISE: James 5:16
Therefore, confess your sins to one another and pray for one another, that you may be healed. The prayer of a righteous person has great power as it is working.

WHAT WILL I DO TO OBEY GOD TODAY?

_____
_____
_____
_____
_____
_____
_____

FACT
Nepal contains Mt. Everest, the tallest mountain in the world at 29,035 feet.

AUGUST 14

Read 2 Corinthians 12:11–21 (older kids)
Read 2 Corinthians 12:19–21 (younger kids)

TODAY'S PRAYER COUNTRY
NEPAL

Many languages in Nepal have no Bible translation to read. Pray for translators to translate the Bible soon.

WHAT DID I LEARN FROM GOD'S WORD?

_____
_____
_____
_____

MONTHLY PRAYER PROMISE: James 5:16
Therefore, confess your sins to one another and pray for one another, that you may be healed. The prayer of a righteous person has great power as it is working.

WHAT WILL I DO TO OBEY GOD TODAY?

_____
_____
_____
_____
_____
_____
_____

ASIA

FACT
Since 1995, communist rebels have been stirring up trouble and have killed 2,000 people.

AUGUST 15

Read 2 Corinthians 13 (older kids)
Read 2 Corinthians 13:11–14 (younger kids)

TODAY'S PRAYER COUNTRY
NETHERLANDS

Many people in the Netherlands use illegal drugs. Pray that they will turn to Jesus Christ for hope.

WHAT DID I LEARN FROM GOD'S WORD?

_____
_____
_____
_____

MONTHLY PRAYER PROMISE: James 5:16
Therefore, confess your sins to one another and pray for one another, that you may be healed. The prayer of a righteous person has great power as it is working.

WHAT WILL I DO TO OBEY GOD TODAY?

_____
_____
_____
_____
_____
_____
_____

EUROPE

FACT
About half of the Netherlands is below sea level, making dikes (earthen dams) important for use of the land.

AUGUST 16

Read Galatians 1 (older kids)
Read Galatians 1:6–10 (younger kids)

TODAY'S PRAYER COUNTRY

NETHERLANDS

Pray that Christians will reach out to the next generation of children here.

WHAT DID I LEARN FROM GOD'S WORD?

_____
_____
_____
_____

MONTHLY PRAYER PROMISE: James 5:16
Therefore, confess your sins to one another and pray for one another, that you may be healed. The prayer of a righteous person has great power as it is working.

WHAT WILL I DO TO OBEY GOD TODAY?

_____
_____
_____
_____
_____
_____
_____

EUROPE

FACT
The Netherlands suffered a brutal invasion by Germany during World War II.

AUGUST 17

Read Galatians 2:1–10 (older kids)
Read Galatians 2:6–10 (younger kids)

TODAY'S PRAYER COUNTRY

NEW ZEALAND

In New Zealand, most people see the church as unimportant. Pray that churches will faithfully reach out to these people.

WHAT DID I LEARN FROM GOD'S WORD?

_____
_____
_____
_____

MONTHLY PRAYER PROMISE: James 5:16
Therefore, confess your sins to one another and pray for one another, that you may be healed. The prayer of a righteous person has great power as it is working.

WHAT WILL I DO TO OBEY GOD TODAY?

_____
_____
_____
_____
_____
_____
_____

AUSTRALASIA

FACT
Eighty percent of the population are Europeans who have settled here in the last 150 years.

AUGUST 18

Read Galatians 2:11–21 (older kids)
Read Galatians 2:15–21 (younger kids)

TODAY'S PRAYER COUNTRY

NEW ZEALAND

Many young people here are leaving the churches. Pray for more kids and teens to come to church.

WHAT DID I LEARN FROM GOD'S WORD?

MONTHLY PRAYER PROMISE: James 5:16
Therefore, confess your sins to one another and pray for one another, that you may be healed. The prayer of a righteous person has great power as it is working.

WHAT WILL I DO TO OBEY GOD TODAY?

AUSTRALASIA

FACT
Fifteen percent of the population consider themselves to be of more than one race.

AUGUST 19

Read Galatians 3:1–14 (older kids)
Read Galatians 3:10–14 (younger kids)

TODAY'S PRAYER COUNTRY

NICARAGUA

Many people have lost their homes and jobs. Pray for God to give them security and a home.

WHAT DID I LEARN FROM GOD'S WORD?

MONTHLY PRAYER PROMISE: James 5:16
Therefore, confess your sins to one another and pray for one another, that you may be healed. The prayer of a righteous person has great power as it is working.

WHAT WILL I DO TO OBEY GOD TODAY?

NORTH AMERICA

FACT
About half of the people in Nicaragua live on one dollar a day.

AUGUST 20

Read Galatians 3:15–29 (older kids)
Read Galatians 3:23–29 (younger kids)

TODAY'S PRAYER COUNTRY
NICARAGUA

Many people in Nicaragua are active Christians. Pray for them to boldly share their faith in Jesus Christ.

WHAT DID I LEARN FROM GOD'S WORD?

MONTHLY PRAYER PROMISE: James 5:16
Therefore, confess your sins to one another and pray for one another, that you may be healed. The prayer of a righteous person has great power as it is working.

WHAT WILL I DO TO OBEY GOD TODAY?

NORTH AMERICA

FACT
Hurricane Mitch hit Nicaragua in 1998 and did $15 billion in damage; 9,000 people died.

AUGUST 21

Read Galatians 4:1–20 (older kids)
Read Galatians 4:1–7 (younger kids)

TODAY'S PRAYER COUNTRY

NIGER

Many people in Niger cannot read. Pray that loving Christian leaders will help them understand who God is.

WHAT DID I LEARN FROM GOD'S WORD?

_____

_____

_____

_____

MONTHLY PRAYER PROMISE: James 5:16
Therefore, confess your sins to one another and pray for one another, that you may be healed. The prayer of a righteous person has great power as it is working.

WHAT WILL I DO TO OBEY GOD TODAY?

_____

_____

_____

_____

_____

_____

AFRICA

FACT
The Niger River, in the south-west, flows through the country's only fertile area.

AUGUST 22

Read Galatians 4:21–31 (older kids)
Read Galatians 4:21–25 (younger kids)

TODAY'S PRAYER COUNTRY
NIGER

Most people in Niger are Muslim. Pray for more missionaries to reach out to these people.

WHAT DID I LEARN FROM GOD'S WORD?

_____
_____
_____
_____

MONTHLY PRAYER PROMISE: James 5:16
Therefore, confess your sins to one another and pray for one another, that you may be healed. The prayer of a righteous person has great power as it is working.

WHAT WILL I DO TO OBEY GOD TODAY?

_____
_____
_____
_____
_____
_____
_____

AFRICA

FACT
Only three percent of the land here can be used for farming since it is so dry in Niger.

AUGUST 23

Read Galatians 5 (older kids)
Read Galatians 5:16–23 (younger kids)

TODAY'S PRAYER COUNTRY

NIGERIA

Pray for northern Nigeria, which is mostly Muslim. Pray that Christians will love the Muslims.

WHAT DID I LEARN FROM GOD'S WORD?

_____
_____
_____
_____

MONTHLY PRAYER PROMISE: James 5:16
Therefore, confess your sins to one another and pray for one another, that you may be healed. The prayer of a righteous person has great power as it is working.

WHAT WILL I DO TO OBEY GOD TODAY?

_____
_____
_____
_____
_____
_____
_____

AFRICA

FACT
As many as 3 million Christians have gathered together to pray in the city of Lagos.

AUGUST 24

Read Galatians 6 (older kids)
Read Galatians 6:1–10 (younger kids)

TODAY'S PRAYER COUNTRY

NIGERIA

Pray for Christian leaders to train and disciple young people.

WHAT DID I LEARN FROM GOD'S WORD?

_____
_____
_____
_____

MONTHLY PRAYER PROMISE: James 5:16
Therefore, confess your sins to one another and pray for one another, that you may be healed. The prayer of a righteous person has great power as it is working.

WHAT WILL I DO TO OBEY GOD TODAY?

_____
_____
_____
_____
_____
_____

AFRICA

FACT
More people live in Nigeria than in any other country on the African continent.

AUGUST 25

Read Ephesians 1 (older kids)
Read Ephesians 1:15–23 (younger kids)

TODAY'S PRAYER COUNTRY
NORWAY

Pray for the growth and maturity of the churches that have been started in Norway.

WHAT DID I LEARN FROM GOD'S WORD?

MONTHLY PRAYER PROMISE: James 5:16
Therefore, confess your sins to one another and pray for one another, that you may be healed. The prayer of a righteous person has great power as it is working.

WHAT WILL I DO TO OBEY GOD TODAY?

EUROPE

FACT
Norway has been independent from Sweden since 1905.

AUGUST 26

Read Ephesians 2 (older kids)
Read Ephesians 2:8–10 (younger kids)

TODAY'S PRAYER COUNTRY

NORWAY

Half of the people in Norway live in the capital city of Oslo. Pray for more gospel witnesses in this city.

WHAT DID I LEARN FROM GOD'S WORD?

_____
_____
_____
_____

MONTHLY PRAYER PROMISE: James 5:16
Therefore, confess your sins to one another and pray for one another, that you may be healed. The prayer of a righteous person has great power as it is working.

WHAT WILL I DO TO OBEY GOD TODAY?

_____
_____
_____
_____
_____
_____
_____

EUROPE

FACT
Eighty-six percent of the people who live in Norway are Lutherans.

AUGUST 27

Read Ephesians 3:1–13 (older kids)
Read Ephesians 3:7–13 (younger kids)

TODAY'S PRAYER COUNTRY

NORTHERN IRELAND

This country has many youth and children. Pray for the young people of Northern Ireland.

WHAT DID I LEARN FROM GOD'S WORD?

_____
_____
_____
_____

MONTHLY PRAYER PROMISE: James 5:16
Therefore, confess your sins to one another and pray for one another, that you may be healed. The prayer of a righteous person has great power as it is working.

WHAT WILL I DO TO OBEY GOD TODAY?

_____
_____
_____
_____
_____
_____
_____

EUROPE

FACT
Forty-one percent of the people who live in Northern Ireland are Catholic.

AUGUST 28

Read Ephesians 3:14–21 (older kids)
Read Ephesians 3:20–21 (younger kids)

TODAY'S PRAYER COUNTRY

NORTHERN IRELAND

Pray for missionaries to teach that Jesus Christ is the only way to heaven, not good works or "being good."

WHAT DID I LEARN FROM GOD'S WORD?

_____

_____

_____

_____

MONTHLY PRAYER PROMISE: James 5:16
Therefore, confess your sins to one another and pray for one another, that you may be healed. The prayer of a righteous person has great power as it is working.

WHAT WILL I DO TO OBEY GOD TODAY?

_____

_____

_____

_____

_____

_____

_____

EUROPE

FACT
Fifty-four percent of the people who live in the rest of Great Britain are Protestant.

AUGUST 29

Read Ephesians 4 (older kids)
Read Ephesians 4:17–27 (younger kids)

TODAY'S PRAYER COUNTRY
OMAN

There are a few churches in Oman that are seeing people saved. Pray for more Bible-believing churches.

WHAT DID I LEARN FROM GOD'S WORD?

_____
_____
_____
_____

MONTHLY PRAYER PROMISE: James 5:16
Therefore, confess your sins to one another and pray for one another, that you may be healed. The prayer of a righteous person has great power as it is working.

WHAT WILL I DO TO OBEY GOD TODAY?

_____
_____
_____
_____
_____
_____
_____

ASIA

FACT
The Albusaidi family has ruled Oman since 1749.

AUGUST 30

TODAY'S PRAYER COUNTRY

PAKISTAN

Churches, pastors, and Muslim-background believers are targets of violence. Pray for them.

WHAT DID I LEARN FROM GOD'S WORD?

_____

_____

_____

_____

MONTHLY PRAYER PROMISE: James 5:16
Therefore, confess your sins to one another and pray for one another, that you may be healed. The prayer of a righteous person has great power as it is working.

WHAT WILL I DO TO OBEY GOD TODAY?

_____

_____

_____

_____

_____

_____

_____

ASIA

FACT
In Pakistan, thirty-nine percent of the people are under age fifteen and only twenty-five percent of them can go to school.

AUGUST 31

Read Ephesians 6 (older kids)
Read Ephesians 6:1–4 (younger kids)

TODAY'S PRAYER COUNTRY
PAKISTAN

Pray for the many children in Pakistan who know nothing about Jesus Christ.

WHAT DID I LEARN FROM GOD'S WORD?

MONTHLY PRAYER PROMISE: James 5:16
Therefore, confess your sins to one another and pray for one another, that you may be healed. The prayer of a righteous person has great power as it is working.

WHAT WILL I DO TO OBEY GOD TODAY?

ASIA

FACT
Forty percent of the government's money is spent on the army and nuclear weapons.

SEPTEMBER 1

Read Philippians 1 (older kids)
Read Philippians 1:3–11 (younger kids)

TODAY'S PRAYER COUNTRY
PALAU

Many people who live here are Roman Catholic and need to understand that salvation is a free gift from God. Pray for them.

WHAT DID I LEARN FROM GOD'S WORD?

MONTHLY PRAYER PROMISE: 1 John 5:14
And this is the confidence that we have toward him, that if we ask anything according to his will he hears us.

WHAT WILL I DO TO OBEY GOD TODAY?

AUSTRALASIA

FACT
Palau is made up of about 200 islands and is located 500 miles southeast of the Philippines.

SEPTEMBER 2

Read Philippians 2:1–11 (older kids)
Read Philippians 2:1–4 (younger kids)

TODAY'S PRAYER COUNTRY
PALESTINIAN STATE

Pray for radical Muslims to understand that Jesus Christ is the way, the truth, and the life.

WHAT DID I LEARN FROM GOD'S WORD?

_____
_____
_____
_____

MONTHLY PRAYER PROMISE: 1 John 5:14
And this is the confidence that we have toward him, that if we ask anything according to his will he hears us.

WHAT WILL I DO TO OBEY GOD TODAY?

_____
_____
_____
_____
_____
_____
_____

ASIA

FACT
The West Bank is located east of Israel and west of Jordan.

SEPTEMBER 3

Read Philippians 2:12–30 (older kids)
Read Philippians 2:12–18 (younger kids)

TODAY'S PRAYER COUNTRY

PANAMA

Pray that believers will have a passion to see this generation come to Christ and live for God.

WHAT DID I LEARN FROM GOD'S WORD?

_____
_____
_____
_____

MONTHLY PRAYER PROMISE: 1 John 5:14
And this is the confidence that we have toward him, that if we ask anything according to his will he hears us.

WHAT WILL I DO TO OBEY GOD TODAY?

_____
_____
_____
_____
_____
_____
_____

NORTH AMERICA

FACT
Before World War I, the US built the Panama Canal to make a direct shipping route from the Caribbean to the Pacific.

SEPTEMBER 4

Read Philippians 3:1–11 (older kids)
Read Philippians 3:8–11 (younger kids)

TODAY'S PRAYER COUNTRY
PANAMA

Because of drug dealers, it is very dangerous to do missionary activity here. Pray for this to change.

WHAT DID I LEARN FROM GOD'S WORD?

_____
_____
_____
_____

MONTHLY PRAYER PROMISE: 1 John 5:14
And this is the confidence that we have toward him, that if we ask anything according to his will he hears us.

WHAT WILL I DO TO OBEY GOD TODAY?

_____
_____
_____
_____
_____
_____

NORTH AMERICA

FACT
In 1989, the US invaded Panama and arrested military dictator General Noriega for smuggling drugs.

SEPTEMBER 5

Read Philippians 3:12–21 (older kids)
Read Philippians 3:12–16 (younger kids)

TODAY'S PRAYER COUNTRY

PARAGUAY

Pray that Christians will develop a vision to reach out to the lost people in Paraguay.

WHAT DID I LEARN FROM GOD'S WORD?

_____
_____
_____
_____

MONTHLY PRAYER PROMISE: 1 John 5:14
And this is the confidence that we have toward him, that if we ask anything according to his will he hears us.

WHAT WILL I DO TO OBEY GOD TODAY?

_____
_____
_____
_____
_____
_____

SOUTH AMERICA

FACT
Paraguay is about the size of California and is completely landlocked.

SEPTEMBER 6

Read Philippians 4 (older kids)
Read Philippians 4:8–13 (younger kids)

TODAY'S PRAYER COUNTRY

PARAGUAY

Pray for more good Bible-teaching churches in Paraguay.

WHAT DID I LEARN FROM GOD'S WORD?

MONTHLY PRAYER PROMISE: 1 John 5:14
And this is the confidence that we have toward him, that if we ask anything according to his will he hears us.

WHAT WILL I DO TO OBEY GOD TODAY?

SOUTH AMERICA

FACT
Ninety percent of the people who live in Paraguay are Catholics.

SEPTEMBER 7

Read Colossians 1:1–14 (older kids)
Read Colossians 1:9–14 (younger kids)

TODAY'S PRAYER COUNTRY

PERU

Pray for Peru's Quechua people to build strong new Bible-believing churches.

WHAT DID I LEARN FROM GOD'S WORD?

_____

_____

_____

_____

MONTHLY PRAYER PROMISE: 1 John 5:14
And this is the confidence that we have toward him, that if we ask anything according to his will he hears us.

WHAT WILL I DO TO OBEY GOD TODAY?

_____

_____

_____

_____

_____

_____

SOUTH AMERICA

FACT
Forty percent of the people in Peru live in extreme poverty.

SEPTEMBER 8

Read Colossians 1:15–29 (older kids)
Read Colossians 1:16–20 (younger kids)

TODAY'S PRAYER COUNTRY

PERU

Because of a war, there are hundreds of widows and thousands of orphans in Peru. Pray for them.

WHAT DID I LEARN FROM GOD'S WORD?

_____
_____
_____
_____

MONTHLY PRAYER PROMISE: 1 John 5:14
And this is the confidence that we have toward him, that if we ask anything according to his will he hears us.

WHAT WILL I DO TO OBEY GOD TODAY?

_____
_____
_____
_____
_____
_____
_____

SOUTH AMERICA

FACT
Peru is almost as big as Alaska.

SEPTEMBER 9

Read Colossians 2:1–15 (older kids)
Read Colossians 2:6–7 (younger kids)

TODAY'S PRAYER COUNTRY

PHILIPPINES

The Filipino churches have sent over 9,000 missionaries around the world; pray for them to continue sending missionaries.

WHAT DID I LEARN FROM GOD'S WORD?

_____
_____
_____
_____

MONTHLY PRAYER PROMISE: 1 John 5:14
And this is the confidence that we have toward him, that if we ask anything according to his will he hears us.

WHAT WILL I DO TO OBEY GOD TODAY?

_____
_____
_____
_____
_____
_____
_____

AUSTRALASIA

FACT
Philippines is made up of about 7,000 islands; only seven percent of the islands are larger than one square mile.

SEPTEMBER 10

Read Colossians 2:16–23 (older kids)
Read Colossians 2:16–19 (younger kids)

TODAY'S PRAYER COUNTRY
PHILIPPINES

There are Christians in leadership in the Filipino government. Pray for them to be wise.

WHAT DID I LEARN FROM GOD'S WORD?

_____
_____
_____
_____

MONTHLY PRAYER PROMISE: 1 John 5:14
And this is the confidence that we have toward him, that if we ask anything according to his will he hears us.

WHAT WILL I DO TO OBEY GOD TODAY?

_____
_____
_____
_____
_____
_____
_____

AUSTRALASIA

FACT
Three hundred thousand Filipino prayer warriors have committed to pray for their country one hour each day.

SEPTEMBER 11

Read Colossians 3 (older kids)
Read Colossians 3:1–4 (younger kids)

TODAY'S PRAYER COUNTRY

POLAND

Crime and violence are on the rise in Poland. Pray for the Polish people to find the Prince of Peace.

WHAT DID I LEARN FROM GOD'S WORD?

_____
_____
_____
_____

MONTHLY PRAYER PROMISE: 1 John 5:14
And this is the confidence that we have toward him, that if we ask anything according to his will he hears us.

WHAT WILL I DO TO OBEY GOD TODAY?

_____
_____
_____
_____
_____
_____
_____

EUROPE

FACT
Poland was a strong supporter of the US and Britain in the Iraq war and sent 200 troops to help.

SEPTEMBER 12

Read Colossians 4 (older kids)
Read Colossians 4:2–6 (younger kids)

TODAY'S PRAYER COUNTRY

POLAND

Many people in Poland are Catholic and believe they can work their way to heaven. Pray for them.

WHAT DID I LEARN FROM GOD'S WORD?

_____
_____
_____
_____

MONTHLY PRAYER PROMISE: 1 John 5:14
And this is the confidence that we have toward him, that if we ask anything according to his will he hears us.

WHAT WILL I DO TO OBEY GOD TODAY?

_____
_____
_____
_____
_____
_____
_____

EUROPE

FACT
In 1980, an electrician named Lech Walesa launched a drive for Polish freedom. He won the Nobel Peace Prize in 1983 and served as president of Poland from 1990–1995.

SEPTEMBER 13

Read 1 Thessalonians 1 (older kids)
Read 1 Thessalonians 1:2–7 (younger kids)

TODAY'S PRAYER COUNTRY

PORTUGAL

One hundred ninety million people worldwide speak Portuguese. Pray for the Portuguese to develop a vision to witness around the world.

WHAT DID I LEARN FROM GOD'S WORD?

MONTHLY PRAYER PROMISE: 1 John 5:14
And this is the confidence that we have toward him, that if we ask anything according to his will he hears us.

WHAT WILL I DO TO OBEY GOD TODAY?

EUROPE

FACT
During the 1500s, Portugal tried to dominate and control the entire world.

SEPTEMBER 14

Read 1 Thessalonians 2:1–8 (older kids)
Read 1 Thessalonians 2:6–8 (younger kids)

TODAY'S PRAYER COUNTRY

QATAR

There are small groups of Christians from many nationalities here. Pray for them to share their faith.

WHAT DID I LEARN FROM GOD'S WORD?

_____

_____

_____

_____

MONTHLY PRAYER PROMISE: 1 John 5:14
And this is the confidence that we have toward him, that if we ask anything according to his will he hears us.

WHAT WILL I DO TO OBEY GOD TODAY?

_____

_____

_____

_____

_____

_____

_____

FACT
Only one in five residents of Qatar were born here. The rest are guest workers from India, Iran, and Africa.

SEPTEMBER 15

Read 1 Thessalonians 2:9–16 (older kids)
Read 1 Thessalonians 2:9–13 (younger kids)

TODAY'S PRAYER COUNTRY

ROMANIA

Pray that Romanians will find hope and freedom in Jesus.

WHAT DID I LEARN FROM GOD'S WORD?

_____

_____

_____

_____

MONTHLY PRAYER PROMISE: 1 John 5:14
And this is the confidence that we have toward him, that if we ask anything according to his will he hears us.

WHAT WILL I DO TO OBEY GOD TODAY?

_____

_____

_____

_____

_____

_____

_____

EUROPE

FACT
Romania has one of the highest abortion rates in the world.

SEPTEMBER 16

Read 1 Thessalonians 3 (older kids)
Read 1 Thessalonians 3:8–13 (younger kids)

TODAY'S PRAYER COUNTRY
ROMANIA

Thousands of children in Romania live in orphanages or on the streets. Pray for these children who have no parents.

WHAT DID I LEARN FROM GOD'S WORD?

_____
_____
_____
_____

MONTHLY PRAYER PROMISE: 1 John 5:14
And this is the confidence that we have toward him, that if we ask anything according to his will he hears us.

WHAT WILL I DO TO OBEY GOD TODAY?

_____
_____
_____
_____
_____
_____
_____

EUROPE

FACT
Transylvania, home to the legendary Count Dracula, is located in Romania.

SEPTEMBER 17

Read 1 Thessalonians 4:1–12 (older kids)
Read 1 Thessalonians 4:1–5 (younger kids)

TODAY'S PRAYER COUNTRY

RUSSIA

There is a high rate of crime, drug abuse, and family breakdown in Russia. Pray for people to come to Jesus Christ.

WHAT DID I LEARN FROM GOD'S WORD?

_____
_____
_____
_____

MONTHLY PRAYER PROMISE: 1 John 5:14
And this is the confidence that we have toward him, that if we ask anything according to his will he hears us.

WHAT WILL I DO TO OBEY GOD TODAY?

_____
_____
_____
_____
_____
_____
_____

ASIA

FACT
Russia is nearly two times the size of the next-largest country, stretching through eleven time zones.

SEPTEMBER 18

Read 1 Thessalonians 4:13–18 (older kids)
Read 1 Thessalonians 4:14–17 (younger kids)

TODAY'S PRAYER COUNTRY

RUSSIA

Children are at high risk in Russia. Pray for them to be loved, cared for, and given a safer future.

WHAT DID I LEARN FROM GOD'S WORD?

_____
_____
_____
_____

MONTHLY PRAYER PROMISE: 1 John 5:14
And this is the confidence that we have toward him, that if we ask anything according to his will he hears us.

WHAT WILL I DO TO OBEY GOD TODAY?

_____
_____
_____
_____
_____
_____
_____

ASIA

FACT
Over 1 million children are living on the streets in Russia.

SEPTEMBER 19

Read 1 Thessalonians 5 (older kids)
Read 1 Thessalonians 5:1–11 (younger kids)

TODAY'S PRAYER COUNTRY

RWANDA

Over 500,000 children in Rwanda are homeless. Pray for them to have a real home.

WHAT DID I LEARN FROM GOD'S WORD?

_____
_____
_____
_____

MONTHLY PRAYER PROMISE: 1 John 5:14
And this is the confidence that we have toward him, that if we ask anything according to his will he hears us.

WHAT WILL I DO TO OBEY GOD TODAY?

_____
_____
_____
_____
_____
_____
_____

AFRICA

FACT
Rwanda's Lake Kivu is the highest lake in all of Africa.

SEPTEMBER 20

Read 2 Thessalonians 1 (older kids)
Read 2 Thessalonians 1:5–10 (younger kids)

TODAY'S PRAYER COUNTRY

RWANDA

The Hutu and the Tutsi tribes literally hate each other. Pray for them to find the love of Jesus.

WHAT DID I LEARN FROM GOD'S WORD?

MONTHLY PRAYER PROMISE: 1 John 5:14
And this is the confidence that we have toward him, that if we ask anything according to his will he hears us.

WHAT WILL I DO TO OBEY GOD TODAY?

FACT
In 1994, in only 100 days, 800,000 Tutsi people were killed by Hutus.

SEPTEMBER 21

Read 2 Thessalonians 2:1–12 (older kids)
Read 2 Thessalonians 2:1–4 (younger kids)

TODAY'S PRAYER COUNTRY
ST. KITTS AND NEVIS

This country is a popular tourist area in the Caribbean. Pray for the churches to reach tourists for Christ.

WHAT DID I LEARN FROM GOD'S WORD?

_____
_____
_____
_____

MONTHLY PRAYER PROMISE: 1 John 5:14
And this is the confidence that we have toward him, that if we ask anything according to his will he hears us.

WHAT WILL I DO TO OBEY GOD TODAY?

_____
_____
_____
_____
_____
_____
_____

NORTH AMERICA

FACT
Christopher Columbus explored St. Kitts and Nevis in 1493.

SEPTEMBER 22

Read 2 Thessalonians 2:13–17 (older kids)
Read 2 Thessalonians 2:13–15 (younger kids)

TODAY'S PRAYER COUNTRY
ST. LUCIA

Pray that Christians will be able to build quality friendships with young people and see them come to know God.

WHAT DID I LEARN FROM GOD'S WORD?

_____
_____
_____
_____

MONTHLY PRAYER PROMISE: 1 John 5:14
And this is the confidence that we have toward him, that if we ask anything according to his will he hears us.

WHAT WILL I DO TO OBEY GOD TODAY?

_____
_____
_____
_____
_____
_____
_____

NORTH AMERICA

FACT
St. Lucia is one of the most beautiful islands in the Caribbean.

SEPTEMBER 23

Read 2 Thessalonians 3 (older kids)
Read 2 Thessalonians 3:1–5 (younger kids)

TODAY'S PRAYER COUNTRY
ST. VINCENT AND THE GRENADINES

Pray that churches will develop a vision to teach the Bible and reach the lost.

WHAT DID I LEARN FROM GOD'S WORD?

_____
_____
_____
_____

MONTHLY PRAYER PROMISE: 1 John 5:14
And this is the confidence that we have toward him, that if we ask anything according to his will he hears us.

WHAT WILL I DO TO OBEY GOD TODAY?

_____
_____
_____
_____
_____
_____
_____

NORTH AMERICA

FACT
The main island of St. Vincent is eighteen miles long and eleven miles wide.

SEPTEMBER 24

Read 1 Timothy 1:1–11 (older kids)
Read 1 Timothy 1:8–11 (younger kids)

TODAY'S PRAYER COUNTRY

SAMOA

Many Samoan Christians read the Bible and pray every day. Pray for these people to disciple others.

WHAT DID I LEARN FROM GOD'S WORD?

_____
_____
_____
_____

MONTHLY PRAYER PROMISE: 1 John 5:14
And this is the confidence that we have toward him, that if we ask anything according to his will he hears us.

WHAT WILL I DO TO OBEY GOD TODAY?

_____
_____
_____
_____
_____
_____
_____

AUSTRALASIA

FACT
New Zealand seized Samoa from Germany in 1914.

SEPTEMBER 25

Read 1 Timothy 1:12–20 (older kids)
Read 1 Timothy 1:18–20 (younger kids)

TODAY'S PRAYER COUNTRY

SAN MARINO

Evangelical Christians have been jailed or forced to leave this country. Pray for there to be a bold witness in San Marino.

WHAT DID I LEARN FROM GOD'S WORD?

_____
_____
_____
_____

MONTHLY PRAYER PROMISE: 1 John 5:14
And this is the confidence that we have toward him, that if we ask anything according to his will he hears us.

WHAT WILL I DO TO OBEY GOD TODAY?

_____
_____
_____
_____
_____
_____
_____

EUROPE

FACT
Located near Italy, San Marino is one-tenth the size of New York City.

SEPTEMBER 26

Read 1 Timothy 2 (older kids)
Read 1 Timothy 2:1–7 (younger kids)

TODAY'S PRAYER COUNTRY

SÃO TOMÉ AND PRINCIPE

Pray that missionaries can train local leaders here to start new churches.

WHAT DID I LEARN FROM GOD'S WORD?

_____
_____
_____
_____

MONTHLY PRAYER PROMISE: 1 John 5:14
And this is the confidence that we have toward him, that if we ask anything according to his will he hears us.

WHAT WILL I DO TO OBEY GOD TODAY?

_____
_____
_____
_____
_____
_____
_____

AFRICA

FACT
São Tomé and Principe are two tiny islands located near western Africa; ninety-five percent of the citizens live on São Tomé.

SEPTEMBER 27

Read 1 Timothy 3:1–7 (older kids)
Read 1 Timothy 3:1–6 (younger kids)

TODAY'S PRAYER COUNTRY

SAUDI ARABIA

If someone in this country believes in Jesus, he or she can be put to death. Pray for the safety of believers.

WHAT DID I LEARN FROM GOD'S WORD?

MONTHLY PRAYER PROMISE: 1 John 5:14
And this is the confidence that we have toward him, that if we ask anything according to his will he hears us.

WHAT WILL I DO TO OBEY GOD TODAY?

ASIA

FACT
Saudi Arabia is home to Islam's holiest city, Mecca.

SEPTEMBER 28

Read 1 Timothy 3:8–16 (older kids)
Read 1 Timothy 3:14–16 (younger kids)

TODAY'S PRAYER COUNTRY
SAUDI ARABIA

Saudi Arabia is one of the least-evangelized countries in the world. Pray for God to open new doors here.

WHAT DID I LEARN FROM GOD'S WORD?

MONTHLY PRAYER PROMISE: 1 John 5:14
And this is the confidence that we have toward him, that if we ask anything according to his will he hears us.

WHAT WILL I DO TO OBEY GOD TODAY?

ASIA

FACT
Five times every day, 1.2 billion Muslims pray towards the Saudi Arabian city of Mecca.

SEPTEMBER 29

Read 1 Timothy 4 (older kids)
Read 1 Timothy 4:6–10 (younger kids)

TODAY'S PRAYER COUNTRY

SCOTLAND

Many churches in Scotland no longer preach the gospel of Jesus Christ. Pray for them.

WHAT DID I LEARN FROM GOD'S WORD?

_____
_____
_____
_____

MONTHLY PRAYER PROMISE: 1 John 5:14
And this is the confidence that we have toward him, that if we ask anything according to his will he hears us.

WHAT WILL I DO TO OBEY GOD TODAY?

_____
_____
_____
_____
_____
_____
_____

EUROPE

FACT
In 1999, Scotland elected its own government for the first time in 300 years.

SEPTEMBER 30

Read 1 Timothy 5 (older kids)
Read 1 Timothy 5:1–8 (younger kids)

TODAY'S PRAYER COUNTRY

SCOTLAND

Scotland needs missionaries very badly.
Pray for missionaries to go there.

WHAT DID I LEARN FROM GOD'S WORD?

_____

_____

_____

_____

MONTHLY PRAYER PROMISE: 1 John 5:14
And this is the confidence that we have toward him, that if we ask anything according to his will he hears us.

WHAT WILL I DO TO OBEY GOD TODAY?

_____

_____

_____

_____

_____

_____

_____

FACT
Scotland occupies the northern third of the island of Great Britain.

OCTOBER 1

Read 1 Timothy 6 (older kids)
Read 1 Timothy 6:11–21 (younger kids)

TODAY'S PRAYER COUNTRY

SENEGAL

There is religious freedom in Senegal despite the fact that it is a Muslim country. Pray for witnesses in Senegal.

WHAT DID I LEARN FROM GOD'S WORD?

_____
_____
_____
_____

MONTHLY PRAYER PROMISE: Psalm 121:2
My help comes from the LORD, who made heaven and earth.

WHAT WILL I DO TO OBEY GOD TODAY?

_____
_____
_____
_____
_____
_____
_____

AFRICA

FACT
Eighty percent of the people who live in Senegal belong to three powerful Muslim groups.

OCTOBER 2

Read 2 Timothy 1 (older kids)
Read 2 Timothy 1:3–7 (younger kids)

TODAY'S PRAYER COUNTRY

SENEGAL

Pray for more full-time Christian workers in Senegal. Only about 100 are there right now.

WHAT DID I LEARN FROM GOD'S WORD?

_____

_____

_____

_____

MONTHLY PRAYER PROMISE: Psalm 121:2
My help comes from the LORD, who made heaven and earth.

WHAT WILL I DO TO OBEY GOD TODAY?

_____

_____

_____

_____

_____

_____

_____

FACT
The best soccer teams on the continent of Africa are usually from Senegal.

OCTOBER 3

Read 2 Timothy 2:1–13 (older kids)
Read 2 Timothy 2:1–7 (younger kids)

TODAY'S PRAYER COUNTRY

SERBIA

In a recent war, many Muslims were cared for by Christians. Pray for them to come to faith in Jesus Christ.

WHAT DID I LEARN FROM GOD'S WORD?

_____
_____
_____
_____

MONTHLY PRAYER PROMISE: Psalm 121:2
My help comes from the LORD, who made heaven and earth.

WHAT WILL I DO TO OBEY GOD TODAY?

_____
_____
_____
_____
_____
_____
_____

EUROPE

FACT
Minority immigrants—mostly Albanians, Hungarians, and Bosnians—make up one-third of Serbia's population.

OCTOBER 4

Read 2 Timothy 2:14–26 (older kids)
Read 2 Timothy 2:22–26 (younger kids)

TODAY'S PRAYER COUNTRY

SERBIA

Pray for Christians to be a good example of love and forgiveness. Many people in this country hate each other.

WHAT DID I LEARN FROM GOD'S WORD?

_____
_____
_____
_____

MONTHLY PRAYER PROMISE: Psalm 121:2
My help comes from the LORD, who made heaven and earth.

WHAT WILL I DO TO OBEY GOD TODAY?

_____
_____
_____
_____
_____
_____
_____

EUROPE

FACT
Serbia and Montenegro were two republics that came from Yugoslavia; in 2006, Montenegro split from Serbia.

OCTOBER 5

Read 2 Timothy 3:1–9 (older kids)
Read 2 Timothy 3:1–5 (younger kids)

TODAY'S PRAYER COUNTRY

SEYCHELLES

Many people here are superstitious and practice magic. Pray for them to come to a real trust in Jesus Christ.

WHAT DID I LEARN FROM GOD'S WORD?

MONTHLY PRAYER PROMISE: Psalm 121:2
My help comes from the LORD, who made heaven and earth.

WHAT WILL I DO TO OBEY GOD TODAY?

AFRICA

FACT
Seychelles consists of about 100 islands in the Indian Ocean northeast of Madagascar.

OCTOBER 6

Read 2 Timothy 3:10–17 (older kids)
Read 2 Timothy 3:15–17 (younger kids)

TODAY'S PRAYER COUNTRY
SEYCHELLES

Pray for Christian radio to reach many people for Christ, even in other countries that listen to their broadcasts.

WHAT DID I LEARN FROM GOD'S WORD?

_____
_____
_____
_____

MONTHLY PRAYER PROMISE: Psalm 121:2
My help comes from the LORD, who made heaven and earth.

WHAT WILL I DO TO OBEY GOD TODAY?

_____
_____
_____
_____
_____
_____
_____

AFRICA

FACT
FEBA, a Christian radio ministry, is based here; it broadcasts in more than fifty languages.

OCTOBER 7

Read 2 Timothy 4 (older kids)
Read 2 Timothy 4:1–5 (younger kids)

TODAY'S PRAYER COUNTRY

SIERRA LEONE

This country was the first West African country to hear the gospel. Pray for more people to hear and follow Christ.

WHAT DID I LEARN FROM GOD'S WORD?

_____
_____
_____
_____

MONTHLY PRAYER PROMISE: Psalm 121:2
My help comes from the LORD, who made heaven and earth.

WHAT WILL I DO TO OBEY GOD TODAY?

_____
_____
_____
_____
_____
_____
_____

AFRICA

FACT
In a recent war, over 6,000 children were forced to fight as soldiers.

OCTOBER 8

Read Titus 1 (older kids)
Read Titus 1:10–16 (younger kids)

TODAY'S PRAYER COUNTRY

SIERRA LEONE

Pray for fresh vision and passion to reach the Muslim people of Sierra Leone. Seventy percent of the people are Muslims.

WHAT DID I LEARN FROM GOD'S WORD?

_____
_____
_____
_____

MONTHLY PRAYER PROMISE: Psalm 121:2
My help comes from the LORD, who made heaven and earth.

WHAT WILL I DO TO OBEY GOD TODAY?

_____
_____
_____
_____
_____
_____
_____

AFRICA

FACT
Access to doctors and hospitals here is the worst in the world.

OCTOBER 9

Read Titus 2:1–10 (older kids)
Read Titus 2:1–5 (younger kids)

TODAY'S PRAYER COUNTRY

SINGAPORE

One-third of the students here are Christians. Pray for them to reach out to other students.

WHAT DID I LEARN FROM GOD'S WORD?

_____

_____

_____

_____

MONTHLY PRAYER PROMISE: Psalm 121:2
My help comes from the LORD, who made heaven and earth.

WHAT WILL I DO TO OBEY GOD TODAY?

_____

_____

_____

_____

_____

_____

_____

AUSTRALASIA

FACT
Most of the country of Singapore is actually one big city of about 3.5 million people.

OCTOBER 10

Read Titus 2:11–15 (older kids)
Read Titus 2:11–14 (younger kids)

TODAY'S PRAYER COUNTRY
SINGAPORE

People in Singapore are considered Muslim by birth. Pray for them to turn to Christ.

WHAT DID I LEARN FROM GOD'S WORD?

_____

_____

_____

_____

MONTHLY PRAYER PROMISE: Psalm 121:2
My help comes from the LORD, who made heaven and earth.

WHAT WILL I DO TO OBEY GOD TODAY?

_____

_____

_____

_____

_____

_____

_____

AUSTRALASIA

FACT
Singapore also includes fifty-eight islands between the South China Sea and the Indian Ocean.

OCTOBER 11

Read Titus 3 (older kids)
Read Titus 3:1–7 (younger kids)

TODAY'S PRAYER COUNTRY

SLOVAKIA

Not many Christian resources are available in Slovakia. Pray for more resources for Slovakians.

WHAT DID I LEARN FROM GOD'S WORD?

MONTHLY PRAYER PROMISE: Psalm 121:2
My help comes from the LORD, who made heaven and earth.

WHAT WILL I DO TO OBEY GOD TODAY?

EUROPE

FACT
In 1989, communism in Slovakia ended without bloodshed or violence, so it became known as the Velvet Revolution.

OCTOBER 12

Read Philemon (older kids)
Read Philemon 8–14 (younger kids)

TODAY'S PRAYER COUNTRY
SLOVAKIA
Pray for more vision for churches to be planted in every community in Slovakia.

WHAT DID I LEARN FROM GOD'S WORD?

_____
_____
_____
_____

MONTHLY PRAYER PROMISE: Psalm 121:2
My help comes from the LORD, who made heaven and earth.

WHAT WILL I DO TO OBEY GOD TODAY?

_____
_____
_____
_____
_____
_____

EUROPE

FACT
In 1993, Czechoslovakia split peacefully into two separate countries, the Czech Republic and Slovakia.

OCTOBER 13

Read Hebrews 1 (older kids)
Read Hebrews 1:1–4 (younger kids)

TODAY'S PRAYER COUNTRY

SLOVENIA

Slovenia has a strong Catholic culture but many people do not know God personally. Pray for them.

WHAT DID I LEARN FROM GOD'S WORD?

_____
_____
_____
_____

MONTHLY PRAYER PROMISE: Psalm 121:2
My help comes from the LORD, who made heaven and earth.

WHAT WILL I DO TO OBEY GOD TODAY?

_____
_____
_____
_____
_____
_____
_____

EUROPE

FACT
Slovenia is the richest of the former Yugoslav republics.

OCTOBER 14

Read Hebrews 2:1–9 (older kids)
Read Hebrews 2:1–4 (younger kids)

TODAY'S PRAYER COUNTRY

SLOVENIA

A Bible translation is now available for people living in Slovenia. Pray for people to read this new translation.

WHAT DID I LEARN FROM GOD'S WORD?

_____
_____
_____
_____

MONTHLY PRAYER PROMISE: Psalm 121:2
My help comes from the LORD, who made heaven and earth.

WHAT WILL I DO TO OBEY GOD TODAY?

_____
_____
_____
_____
_____
_____
_____

EUROPE

FACT
Slovenia gained its independence in 1991.

OCTOBER 15

Read Hebrews 2:10–18 (older kids)
Read Hebrews 2:14–18 (younger kids)

TODAY'S PRAYER COUNTRY

SOLOMON ISLANDS

Pray that there would be an end to all tension between the different islands of this country. The Prince of Peace can make this happen.

WHAT DID I LEARN FROM GOD'S WORD?

MONTHLY PRAYER PROMISE: Psalm 121:2
My help comes from the LORD, who made heaven and earth.

WHAT WILL I DO TO OBEY GOD TODAY?

AUSTRALASIA

FACT
There are about 1,000 islands in this country, which is located in the Pacific Ocean.

OCTOBER 16

Read Hebrews 3:1–6 (older kids)
Read Hebrews 3:1–3 (younger kids)

TODAY'S PRAYER COUNTRY

SOLOMON ISLANDS

Pray that people from each generation will come to have a personal relationship with Jesus Christ.

WHAT DID I LEARN FROM GOD'S WORD?

_____
_____
_____
_____

MONTHLY PRAYER PROMISE: Psalm 121:2
My help comes from the LORD, who made heaven and earth.

WHAT WILL I DO TO OBEY GOD TODAY?

_____
_____
_____
_____
_____
_____
_____

AUSTRALASIA

FACT
Some of the bloodiest battles of WWII were fought here, most notably the battle at Guadalcanal.

OCTOBER 17

Read Hebrews 3:7–19 (older kids)
Read Hebrews 3:7–11 (younger kids)

TODAY'S PRAYER COUNTRY

SOMALIA

Christians are being forced out of Somalia and very few remain. Pray for those who are left.

WHAT DID I LEARN FROM GOD'S WORD?

_____
_____
_____
_____

MONTHLY PRAYER PROMISE: Psalm 121:2
My help comes from the LORD, who made heaven and earth.

WHAT WILL I DO TO OBEY GOD TODAY?

_____
_____
_____
_____
_____
_____
_____

AFRICA

FACT
By law, all Muslim children have to attend Islam classes, even if they are students in private Christian schools.

OCTOBER 18

Read Hebrews 4:1–13 (older kids)
Read Hebrews 4:6–13 (younger kids)

TODAY'S PRAYER COUNTRY
SOMALIA

This country has known a great deal of poverty and war. Pray for God to break through in Somalia.

WHAT DID I LEARN FROM GOD'S WORD?

_____
_____
_____
_____

MONTHLY PRAYER PROMISE: Psalm 121:2
My help comes from the LORD, who made heaven and earth.

WHAT WILL I DO TO OBEY GOD TODAY?

_____
_____
_____
_____
_____
_____
_____

AFRICA

FACT
Drug lords fight for control of this land by selling drugs and guns.

OCTOBER 19

Read Hebrews 4:14–5:10 (older kids)
Read Hebrews 4:14–16 (younger kids)

TODAY'S PRAYER COUNTRY

SOUTH AFRICA

One-third of the teachers here are HIV positive. Pray for these teachers to become followers of Christ if they don't already know Him.

WHAT DID I LEARN FROM GOD'S WORD?

_____
_____
_____
_____

MONTHLY PRAYER PROMISE: Psalm 121:2
My help comes from the LORD, who made heaven and earth.

WHAT WILL I DO TO OBEY GOD TODAY?

_____
_____
_____
_____
_____
_____
_____

AFRICA

FACT
In South Africa, the murder rate is seven times higher than that of the United States.

OCTOBER 20

Read Hebrews 5:11–6:12 (older kids)
Read Hebrews 5:11–14 (younger kids)

TODAY'S PRAYER COUNTRY
SOUTH AFRICA

Nearly half the people are under age twenty; many are looking for answers. Pray for them to come to Christ.

WHAT DID I LEARN FROM GOD'S WORD?

_____
_____
_____
_____

MONTHLY PRAYER PROMISE: Psalm 121:2
My help comes from the LORD, who made heaven and earth.

WHAT WILL I DO TO OBEY GOD TODAY?

_____
_____
_____
_____
_____
_____
_____

AFRICA

FACT
From 1948 until the late 1980s, South Africa practiced apartheid (strict racial segregation).

OCTOBER 21

Read Hebrews 6:13–20 (older kids)
Read Hebrews 6:16–20 (younger kids)

TODAY'S PRAYER COUNTRY
SPAIN

There are more AIDS victims in Spain than anywhere else in Europe. Pray for these people to find help.

WHAT DID I LEARN FROM GOD'S WORD?

_____
_____
_____
_____

MONTHLY PRAYER PROMISE: Psalm 121:2
My help comes from the LORD, who made heaven and earth.

WHAT WILL I DO TO OBEY GOD TODAY?

_____
_____
_____
_____
_____
_____
_____

EUROPE

FACT
Spain occupies eighty-five percent of the Iberian peninsula, which it shares with Portugal.

OCTOBER 22

Read Hebrews 7:1–10 (older kids)
Read Hebrews 7:1–3 (younger kids)

TODAY'S PRAYER COUNTRY

SPAIN

Pray that missionaries in Spain will be able to build strong, Bible-believing churches.

WHAT DID I LEARN FROM GOD'S WORD?

_____
_____
_____
_____

MONTHLY PRAYER PROMISE: Psalm 121:2
My help comes from the LORD, who made heaven and earth.

WHAT WILL I DO TO OBEY GOD TODAY?

_____
_____
_____
_____
_____
_____
_____

EUROPE

FACT
Africa is less than ten miles south of Spain at the Strait of Gibraltar.

OCTOBER 23

Read Hebrews 7:11–28 (older kids)
Read Hebrews 7:22–28 (younger kids)

TODAY'S PRAYER COUNTRY

SRI LANKA

Pray for the many children and adults who have experienced the pain and terror of war.

WHAT DID I LEARN FROM GOD'S WORD?

_____
_____
_____
_____

MONTHLY PRAYER PROMISE: Psalm 121:2
My help comes from the LORD, who made heaven and earth.

WHAT WILL I DO TO OBEY GOD TODAY?

_____
_____
_____
_____
_____
_____
_____

ASIA

FACT
Children as young as fourteen have been used to fight for an extremist group, the Tamil Tigers.

OGTOBER 24

Read Hebrews 8 (older kids)
Read Hebrews 8:8–12 (younger kids)

TODAY'S PRAYER COUNTRY

SRI LANKA

Pray for witnesses in the many villages that have no gospel witness.

WHAT DID I LEARN FROM GOD'S WORD?

MONTHLY PRAYER PROMISE: Psalm 121:2
My help comes from the LORD, who made heaven and earth.

WHAT WILL I DO TO OBEY GOD TODAY?

ASIA

FACT
Thirty-five-thousand villages in Sri Lanka have no contact with any Christians.

OCTOBER 25

Read Hebrews 9:1–10 (older kids)
Read Hebrews 9:6–10 (younger kids)

TODAY'S PRAYER COUNTRY
SUDAN

The Islamic government of Sudan has brought back slavery. Pray that this evil practice will stop.

WHAT DID I LEARN FROM GOD'S WORD?

_____
_____
_____
_____

MONTHLY PRAYER PROMISE: Psalm 121:2
My help comes from the LORD, who made heaven and earth.

WHAT WILL I DO TO OBEY GOD TODAY?

_____
_____
_____
_____
_____
_____
_____

AFRICA

FACT
Sudan is the largest country on the continent of Africa; it is one-fourth the size of the US.

OCTOBER 26

Read Hebrews 9:11–28 (older kids)
Read Hebrews 9:23–28 (younger kids)

TODAY'S PRAYER COUNTRY

SUDAN

Churches have been bombed in Sudan. Pray for the believers in this area to be able to worship the Lord Jesus safely.

WHAT DID I LEARN FROM GOD'S WORD?

_____

_____

_____

_____

MONTHLY PRAYER PROMISE: Psalm 121:2
My help comes from the LORD, who made heaven and earth.

WHAT WILL I DO TO OBEY GOD TODAY?

_____

_____

_____

_____

_____

_____

_____

AFRICA

FACT
In 2003, conflict began in the Darfur region of western Sudan. Millions have been affected.

OCTOBER 27

Read Hebrews 10:1–18 (older kids)
Read Hebrews 10:1–7 (younger kids)

TODAY'S PRAYER COUNTRY

SURINAME

Many young people here are turning to God. Pray that they will remain committed to God in their daily lives.

WHAT DID I LEARN FROM GOD'S WORD?

_____
_____
_____
_____

MONTHLY PRAYER PROMISE: Psalm 121:2
My help comes from the LORD, who made heaven and earth.

WHAT WILL I DO TO OBEY GOD TODAY?

_____
_____
_____
_____
_____
_____
_____

SOUTH AMERICA

FACT
After 300 years of Dutch rule, Suriname became independent in 1975.

OCTOBER 28

Read Hebrews 10:19–39 (older kids)
Read Hebrews 10:19–25 (younger kids)

TODAY'S PRAYER COUNTRY

SURINAME

Pray for those who call themselves Christians but do not have a personal relationship with Jesus Christ.

WHAT DID I LEARN FROM GOD'S WORD?

MONTHLY PRAYER PROMISE: Psalm 121:2
My help comes from the LORD, who made heaven and earth.

WHAT WILL I DO TO OBEY GOD TODAY?

SOUTH AMERICA

FACT
Nearly half of the people of this country would call themselves Christians.

OCTOBER 29

Read Hebrews 11:1–22 (older kids)
Read Hebrews 11:1–6 (younger kids)

TODAY'S PRAYER COUNTRY

SWAZILAND

Many people in Swaziland worship the dead. Pray that they will worship the Lord Jesus Christ.

WHAT DID I LEARN FROM GOD'S WORD?

_____
_____
_____
_____

MONTHLY PRAYER PROMISE: Psalm 121:2
My help comes from the LORD, who made heaven and earth.

WHAT WILL I DO TO OBEY GOD TODAY?

_____
_____
_____
_____
_____
_____
_____

AFRICA

FACT
Swaziland, which is about 85% the size of New Jersey, is surrounded by South Africa and Mozambique.

OCTOBER 30

Read Hebrews 11:23–40 (older kids)
Read Hebrews 11:23–31 (younger kids)

TODAY'S PRAYER COUNTRY

SWAZILAND

Pray for the many Christians in this country to live dedicated Christian lives.

WHAT DID I LEARN FROM GOD'S WORD?

_____
_____
_____
_____

MONTHLY PRAYER PROMISE: Psalm 121:2
My help comes from the LORD, who made heaven and earth.

WHAT WILL I DO TO OBEY GOD TODAY?

_____
_____
_____
_____
_____
_____
_____

AFRICA

FACT
Over half of the people live in poverty and one-fourth have the AIDS virus.

OCTOBER 31

Read Hebrews 12 (older kids)
Read Hebrews 12:1–3 (younger kids)

TODAY'S PRAYER COUNTRY
SWEDEN

Many Swedish people do not think God is important. Pray for them to recognize the lordship of Jesus Christ.

WHAT DID I LEARN FROM GOD'S WORD?

_____
_____
_____
_____

MONTHLY PRAYER PROMISE: Psalm 121:2
My help comes from the LORD, who made heaven and earth.

WHAT WILL I DO TO OBEY GOD TODAY?

_____
_____
_____
_____
_____
_____
_____

EUROPE

FACT
Sweden is the country that brought us Volvos, Ericsson phones, and IKEA.

NOVEMBER 1

Read Hebrews 13 (older kids)
Read Hebrews 13:7–17 (younger kids)

TODAY'S PRAYER COUNTRY

SWEDEN

Pray that more people from Sweden will be called and trained to serve the Lord.

WHAT DID I LEARN FROM GOD'S WORD?

_____
_____
_____
_____

MONTHLY PRAYER PROMISE: 1 Peter 5:7
Casting all your anxieties on him, because he cares for you.

WHAT WILL I DO TO OBEY GOD TODAY?

_____
_____
_____
_____
_____
_____
_____

EUROPE

FACT
Sweden is the fourth-largest country in Europe and is even larger than California.

NOVEMBER 2

Read James 1 (older kids)
Read James 1:2–12 (younger kids)

TODAY'S PRAYER COUNTRY

SWITZERLAND

A lot of people here live comfortable lives without God. Pray for these people to understand their need for God.

WHAT DID I LEARN FROM GOD'S WORD?

_____
_____
_____
_____

MONTHLY PRAYER PROMISE: 1 Peter 5:7
Casting all your anxieties on him, because he cares for you.

WHAT WILL I DO TO OBEY GOD TODAY?

_____
_____
_____
_____
_____
_____
_____

EUROPE

FACT
Switzerland has remained neutral for every major European conflict since 1815.

NOVEMBER 3

Read James 2 (older kids)
Read James 2:14–26 (younger kids)

TODAY'S PRAYER COUNTRY
SWITZERLAND

There is a growing Christian youth movement here. Pray for these youth to be discipled.

WHAT DID I LEARN FROM GOD'S WORD?

_____
_____
_____
_____

MONTHLY PRAYER PROMISE: 1 Peter 5:7
Casting all your anxieties on him, because he cares for you.

WHAT WILL I DO TO OBEY GOD TODAY?

_____
_____
_____
_____
_____
_____
_____

EUROPE

FACT
Switzerland is one of the world's richest nations.

NOVEMBER 4

Read James 3 (older kids)
Read James 3:1–5 (younger kids)

TODAY'S PRAYER COUNTRY

SYRIA

Any attempt by Christians to share their faith with Muslims is seen as a threat. Pray for wisdom for these Christians.

WHAT DID I LEARN FROM GOD'S WORD?

_____
_____
_____
_____

MONTHLY PRAYER PROMISE: 1 Peter 5:7
Casting all your anxieties on him, because he cares for you.

WHAT WILL I DO TO OBEY GOD TODAY?

_____
_____
_____
_____
_____
_____
_____

ASIA

FACT
Syria has been independent from France since 1946.

NOVEMBER 5

Read James 4 (older kids)
Read James 4:1–8 (younger kids)

TODAY'S PRAYER COUNTRY

SYRIA

Christians here have some freedom to worship. Pray that Syrians will be able to continue to worship Jesus Christ.

WHAT DID I LEARN FROM GOD'S WORD?

_____
_____
_____
_____

MONTHLY PRAYER PROMISE: 1 Peter 5:7
Casting all your anxieties on him, because he cares for you.

WHAT WILL I DO TO OBEY GOD TODAY?

_____
_____
_____
_____
_____
_____
_____

ASIA

FACT
The highest point in Syria is Mount Hermon (9,232 ft.) on the Lebanese border.

NOVEMBER 6

Read James 5:1–12 (older kids)
Read James 5:7–12 (younger kids)

TODAY'S PRAYER COUNTRY

TAIWAN

Many rural churches in Taiwan do not have a pastor. Pray for more trained leaders to pastor these churches.

WHAT DID I LEARN FROM GOD'S WORD?

_____
_____
_____
_____

MONTHLY PRAYER PROMISE: 1 Peter 5:7
Casting all your anxieties on him, because he cares for you.

WHAT WILL I DO TO OBEY GOD TODAY?

_____
_____
_____
_____
_____
_____

FACT
The Chinese government, which rules Taiwan, officially became Communist in 1949.

NOVEMBER 7

Read James 5:13–20 (older kids)
Read James 5:16–20 (younger kids)

TODAY'S PRAYER COUNTRY

TAIWAN

Pray for there to be a real breakthrough by God among the Han Chinese, a people group in Taiwan.

WHAT DID I LEARN FROM GOD'S WORD?

_____

_____

_____

_____

MONTHLY PRAYER PROMISE: 1 Peter 5:7
Casting all your anxieties on him, because he cares for you.

WHAT WILL I DO TO OBEY GOD TODAY?

_____

_____

_____

_____

_____

_____

ASIA

FACT
Most people in Taiwan follow a mix of Confucianism, Buddhism, and Taoism.

NOVEMBER 8

Read 1 Peter 1:1–12 (older kids)
Read 1 Peter 1:10–12 (younger kids)

TODAY'S PRAYER COUNTRY
TAJIKISTAN

Ninety percent of the people here claim to be Muslim, but some are open to hearing about Jesus. Pray for them to welcome the Good News.

WHAT DID I LEARN FROM GOD'S WORD?

_____
_____
_____
_____

MONTHLY PRAYER PROMISE: 1 Peter 5:7
Casting all your anxieties on him, because he cares for you.

WHAT WILL I DO TO OBEY GOD TODAY?

_____
_____
_____
_____
_____
_____
_____

ASIA

FACT
After Tajikistan gained independence from the Soviet Union in 1991, civil war broke out.

NOVEMBER 9

Read 1 Peter 1:13–25 (older kids)
Read 1 Peter 1:22–25 (younger kids)

TODAY'S PRAYER COUNTRY

TAJIKISTAN

Thousands of people lost their homes in the recent civil war. Pray for them to find a home on earth and in heaven.

WHAT DID I LEARN FROM GOD'S WORD?

_____
_____
_____
_____

MONTHLY PRAYER PROMISE: 1 Peter 5:7
Casting all your anxieties on him, because he cares for you.

WHAT WILL I DO TO OBEY GOD TODAY?

_____
_____
_____
_____
_____
_____
_____

ASIA

FACT
Ninety-three percent of the land in Tajikistan is mountainous.

NOVEMBER 10

Read 1 Peter 2:1–12 (older kids)
Read 1 Peter 2:9–12 (younger kids)

TODAY'S PRAYER COUNTRY
TANZANIA

More than a million children in Tanzania are orphans. Pray for these children to be given a home and foster parents.

WHAT DID I LEARN FROM GOD'S WORD?

MONTHLY PRAYER PROMISE: 1 Peter 5:7
Casting all your anxieties on him, because he cares for you.

WHAT WILL I DO TO OBEY GOD TODAY?

AFRICA

FACT
Tanzania is home to Mt. Kilimanjaro, Africa's highest mountain peak.

NOVEMBER 11

Read 1 Peter 3 (older kids)
Read 1 Peter 3:18–22 (younger kids)

TODAY'S PRAYER COUNTRY

TANZANIA

Over 5 million people here listen to Christian radio. Pray for the gospel to go out from these radio stations.

WHAT DID I LEARN FROM GOD'S WORD?

_____
_____
_____
_____

MONTHLY PRAYER PROMISE: 1 Peter 5:7
Casting all your anxieties on him, because he cares for you.

WHAT WILL I DO TO OBEY GOD TODAY?

_____
_____
_____
_____
_____
_____
_____

AFRICA

FACT
One-third of Tanzania is a national park that draws thousands of tourists every year.

NOVEMBER 12

Read 1 Peter 4:1–11 (older kids)
Read 1 Peter 4:7–11 (younger kids)

TODAY'S PRAYER COUNTRY

THAILAND

Pray for the many young Thai girls who are kidnapped and sold into prostitution.

WHAT DID I LEARN FROM GOD'S WORD?

_____
_____
_____
_____

MONTHLY PRAYER PROMISE: 1 Peter 5:7
Casting all your anxieties on him, because he cares for you.

WHAT WILL I DO TO OBEY GOD TODAY?

_____
_____
_____
_____
_____
_____
_____

ASIA

FACT
Twenty percent of all Thai girls between eleven and seventeen years of age are prostitutes.

NOVEMBER 13

Read 1 Peter 4:12–19 (older kids)
Read 1 Peter 4:16–19 (younger kids)

TODAY'S PRAYER COUNTRY

THAILAND

Thailand means "land of the free."
Pray that the Thai people will find
true freedom in Jesus Christ.

WHAT DID I LEARN FROM GOD'S WORD?

_____
_____
_____
_____

MONTHLY PRAYER PROMISE: 1 Peter 5:7
Casting all your anxieties on him, because he cares for you.

WHAT WILL I DO TO OBEY GOD TODAY?

_____
_____
_____
_____
_____
_____
_____

ASIA

FACT
At the beginning of World War II,
Japan attacked Thailand which
resisted for only five hours.

NOVEMBER 14

Read 1 Peter 5 (older kids)
Read 1 Peter 5:5–11 (younger kids)

TODAY'S PRAYER COUNTRY

TOGO

Pray for Christian leaders to be trained and supported by local churches in Togo.

WHAT DID I LEARN FROM GOD'S WORD?

_____
_____
_____
_____

MONTHLY PRAYER PROMISE: 1 Peter 5:7
Casting all your anxieties on him, because he cares for you.

WHAT WILL I DO TO OBEY GOD TODAY?

_____
_____
_____
_____
_____
_____
_____

AFRICA

FACT
Togo is sandwiched between Ghana and Benin in West Africa.

NOVEMBER 15

Read 2 Peter 1:1–15 (older kids)
Read 2 Peter 1:3–11 (younger kids)

TODAY'S PRAYER COUNTRY

TOGO

Many children here have never had an adequate teacher. Pray for the training of teachers that is going on right now.

WHAT DID I LEARN FROM GOD'S WORD?

_____
_____
_____
_____

MONTHLY PRAYER PROMISE: 1 Peter 5:7
Casting all your anxieties on him, because he cares for you.

WHAT WILL I DO TO OBEY GOD TODAY?

_____
_____
_____
_____
_____
_____
_____
_____

AFRICA

FACT
Coffee and cocoa are the main crops produced in Togo.

NOVEMBER 16

Read 2 Peter 1:16–21 (older kids)
Read 2 Peter 1:19–21 (younger kids)

TODAY'S PRAYER COUNTRY

TONGA

Pray for the Tongan church to continue to develop a sense of mission.

WHAT DID I LEARN FROM GOD'S WORD?

_____

_____

_____

_____

MONTHLY PRAYER PROMISE: 1 Peter 5:7
Casting all your anxieties on him, because he cares for you.

WHAT WILL I DO TO OBEY GOD TODAY?

_____

_____

_____

_____

_____

_____

AUSTRALASIA

FACT
Tonga is made up of 171 islands in the south Pacific; people live on thirty-six of these islands.

NOVEMBER 17

Read 2 Peter 2 (older kids)
Read 2 Peter 2:17–22 (younger kids)

TODAY'S PRAYER COUNTRY

TONGA

The growing Chinese population on Tonga is the only unreached people group here. Pray for them.

WHAT DID I LEARN FROM GOD'S WORD?

_____

_____

_____

_____

MONTHLY PRAYER PROMISE: 1 Peter 5:7
Casting all your anxieties on him, because he cares for you.

WHAT WILL I DO TO OBEY GOD TODAY?

_____

_____

_____

_____

_____

_____

_____

AUSTRALASIA

FACT
Captain James Cook landed in these islands in 1773 and nicknamed them the "Friendly Islands."

NOVEMBER 18

Read 2 Peter 3:1–13 (older kids)
Read 2 Peter 3:8–10 (younger kids)

TODAY'S PRAYER COUNTRY

TRINIDAD AND TOBAGO

Pray for the churches on these islands to reach out to lost people.

WHAT DID I LEARN FROM GOD'S WORD?

_____
_____
_____
_____

MONTHLY PRAYER PROMISE: 1 Peter 5:7
Casting all your anxieties on him, because he cares for you.

WHAT WILL I DO TO OBEY GOD TODAY?

_____
_____
_____
_____
_____
_____
_____

SOUTH AMERICA

FACT
The two islands of Trinidad and Tobago are the southernmost of the Winward Islands.

NOVEMBER 19

Read 2 Peter 3:14–18 (older kids)
Read 2 Peter 3:14–18 (younger kids)

TODAY'S PRAYER COUNTRY

TRINIDAD AND TOBAGO

Pray for pastors to be trained and equipped to lead the churches in Trinidad and Tobago.

WHAT DID I LEARN FROM GOD'S WORD?

_____
_____
_____
_____

MONTHLY PRAYER PROMISE: 1 Peter 5:7
Casting all your anxieties on him, because he cares for you.

WHAT WILL I DO TO OBEY GOD TODAY?

_____
_____
_____
_____
_____
_____
_____

SOUTH AMERICA

FACT
These islands were explored by Christopher Columbus in 1498.

NOVEMBER 20

Read 1 John 1 (older kids)
Read 1 John 1:5–10 (younger kids)

TODAY'S PRAYER COUNTRY

TUNISIA

Tunisia is a Muslim country; there is much emptiness in the people. Pray for Tunisians to find God.

WHAT DID I LEARN FROM GOD'S WORD?

_____
_____
_____
_____

MONTHLY PRAYER PROMISE: 1 Peter 5:7
Casting all your anxieties on him, because he cares for you.

WHAT WILL I DO TO OBEY GOD TODAY?

_____
_____
_____
_____
_____
_____
_____

AFRICA

FACT
Kairouan, Tunisia, is considered the fourth holiest city in Islam.

NOVEMBER 21

Read 1 John 2:1–14 (older kids)
Read 1 John 2:1–6 (younger kids)

TODAY'S PRAYER COUNTRY

TUNISIA

Pray for supernatural opportunities for people to find Jesus in this Muslim country.

WHAT DID I LEARN FROM GOD'S WORD?

_____
_____
_____
_____

MONTHLY PRAYER PROMISE: 1 Peter 5:7
Casting all your anxieties on him, because he cares for you.

WHAT WILL I DO TO OBEY GOD TODAY?

_____
_____
_____
_____
_____
_____
_____

AFRICA

FACT
Parts of the Star Wars movies were filmed in Tunisia.

NOVEMBER 22

Read 1 John 2:15–27 (older kids)
Read 1 John 2:15–17 (younger kids)

TODAY'S PRAYER COUNTRY

TURKEY

Pray for the 66 million Muslims in Turkey; most of them do not even know who Jesus is.

WHAT DID I LEARN FROM GOD'S WORD?

_____

_____

_____

_____

MONTHLY PRAYER PROMISE: 1 Peter 5:7
Casting all your anxieties on him, because he cares for you.

WHAT WILL I DO TO OBEY GOD TODAY?

_____

_____

_____

_____

_____

_____

_____

ASIA

FACT
Some have called Turkey the largest unreached country in the world.

NOVEMBER 23

Read 1 John 3:1–10 (older kids)
Read 1 John 3:4–10 (younger kids)

TODAY'S PRAYER COUNTRY

TURKEY

People who decide to follow Jesus are threatened, intimidated, and rejected by their family and others. Pray for them.

WHAT DID I LEARN FROM GOD'S WORD?

_____
_____
_____
_____

MONTHLY PRAYER PROMISE: 1 Peter 5:7
Casting all your anxieties on him, because he cares for you.

WHAT WILL I DO TO OBEY GOD TODAY?

_____
_____
_____
_____
_____
_____

ASIA

FACT
In 1974, Turkey invaded Cyprus. Turkey now controls forty percent of this island.

NOVEMBER 24

Read 1 John 3:11–24 (older kids)
Read 1 John 3:16–24 (younger kids)

TODAY'S PRAYER COUNTRY

TURKMENISTAN

All religion was banned under communism, but now Islam has grown important here. Pray for these people to come to Christ.

WHAT DID I LEARN FROM GOD'S WORD?

_____
_____
_____
_____

MONTHLY PRAYER PROMISE: 1 Peter 5:7
Casting all your anxieties on him, because he cares for you.

WHAT WILL I DO TO OBEY GOD TODAY?

_____
_____
_____
_____
_____
_____

FACT
Turkmenistan, formerly Turkmenia, has one of the world's largest sand deserts.

NOVEMBER 25

Read 1 John 4 (older kids)
Read 1 John 4:7–12 (younger kids)

TODAY'S PRAYER COUNTRY

TURKMENISTAN

Persecution against Christians is on the increase here. Pray for believers to remain faithful to God.

WHAT DID I LEARN FROM GOD'S WORD?

_____
_____
_____
_____

MONTHLY PRAYER PROMISE: 1 Peter 5:7
Casting all your anxieties on him, because he cares for you.

WHAT WILL I DO TO OBEY GOD TODAY?

_____
_____
_____
_____
_____
_____
_____

ASIA

FACT
Turkmenistan is the second-largest Central Asian country.

NOVEMBER 26

Read 1 John 5 (older kids)
Read 1 John 5:10–15 (younger kids)

TODAY'S PRAYER COUNTRY

TUVALU

People of Tuvalu are committed to being friendly. Pray that they will find Jesus to be their best friend ever.

WHAT DID I LEARN FROM GOD'S WORD?

_____
_____
_____
_____

MONTHLY PRAYER PROMISE: 1 Peter 5:7
Casting all your anxieties on him, because he cares for you.

WHAT WILL I DO TO OBEY GOD TODAY?

_____
_____
_____
_____
_____
_____

AUSTRALASIA

FACT
Tuvalu consists of nine tiny islands in the Pacific Ocean, south of the equator.

NOVEMBER 27

Read 2 John (older kids)
Read 2 John 4–11 (younger kids)

TODAY'S PRAYER COUNTRY

TUVALU

The capital city has only five thousand people, but they also need Jesus Christ. Pray for them to come to Christ.

WHAT DID I LEARN FROM GOD'S WORD?

_____
_____
_____
_____

MONTHLY PRAYER PROMISE: 1 Peter 5:7
Casting all your anxieties on him, because he cares for you.

WHAT WILL I DO TO OBEY GOD TODAY?

_____
_____
_____
_____
_____
_____
_____

AUSTRALASIA

FACT
In 1979 the US gave Tuvalu four islands that had formerly been US territory.

NOVEMBER 28

Read 3 John (older kids)
Read 3 John 5–12 (younger kids)

TODAY'S PRAYER COUNTRY

UGANDA

Ten thousand children here have been abducted or stolen. Pray that they would be freed.

WHAT DID I LEARN FROM GOD'S WORD?

_____
_____
_____
_____

MONTHLY PRAYER PROMISE: 1 Peter 5:7
Casting all your anxieties on him, because he cares for you.

WHAT WILL I DO TO OBEY GOD TODAY?

_____
_____
_____
_____
_____
_____

AFRICA

FACT
Idi Amin was the dictator of Uganda in the 1970s and 1980s, during which time many people were murdered.

NOVEMBER 29

Read Jude 1–16 (older kids)
Read Jude 14–16 (younger kids)

TODAY'S PRAYER COUNTRY

UGANDA

Pray for humility, maturity, and a closeness to God in Ugandan church leaders.

WHAT DID I LEARN FROM GOD'S WORD?

_____

_____

_____

_____

MONTHLY PRAYER PROMISE: 1 Peter 5:7
Casting all your anxieties on him, because he cares for you.

WHAT WILL I DO TO OBEY GOD TODAY?

_____

_____

_____

_____

_____

_____

_____

AFRICA

FACT
Uganda has slowed the spread of the AIDS virus more than any other country in the world.

NOVEMBER 30

Read Jude 17–25 (older kids)
Read Jude 17–23 (younger kids)

TODAY'S PRAYER COUNTRY
UKRAINE

Pray for church-planting efforts in Ukraine to be successful. Many new churches are needed.

WHAT DID I LEARN FROM GOD'S WORD?

_____
_____
_____
_____

MONTHLY PRAYER PROMISE: 1 Peter 5:7
Casting all your anxieties on him, because he cares for you.

WHAT WILL I DO TO OBEY GOD TODAY?

_____
_____
_____
_____
_____
_____
_____

EUROPE

FACT
On April 26, 1986, Chernobyl, Ukraine, became the site of the world's worst nuclear disaster.

DECEMBER 1

Read Revelation 1:1–8 (older kids)
Read Revelation 1:4–8 (younger kids)

TODAY'S PRAYER COUNTRY

UKRAINE

Pray that there will be greater freedom for people to hear about Jesus.

WHAT DID I LEARN FROM GOD'S WORD?

_____
_____
_____
_____

MONTHLY PRAYER PROMISE: Deuteronomy 4:29
But from there you will seek the LORD your God and you will find him, if you search after him with all your heart and with all your soul.

WHAT WILL I DO TO OBEY GOD TODAY?

_____
_____
_____
_____
_____
_____
_____

EUROPE

FACT
In June 1996, the last nuclear warhead was removed from Ukraine and taken to Russia.

DECEMBER 2

Read Revelation 1:9–20 (older kids)
Read Revelation 1:17–20 (younger kids)

TODAY'S PRAYER COUNTRY
UNITED ARAB EMIRATES

Some Christians here have been arrested for sharing their faith. Pray for them to continue despite the danger.

WHAT DID I LEARN FROM GOD'S WORD?

_____
_____
_____
_____

MONTHLY PRAYER PROMISE: Deuteronomy 4:29
But from there you will seek the LORD your God and you will find him, if you search after him with all your heart and with all your soul.

WHAT WILL I DO TO OBEY GOD TODAY?

_____
_____
_____
_____
_____
_____
_____

ASIA

FACT
The United Arab Emirates is a collection of seven mini-monarchies.

DECEMBER 3

Read Revelation 2:1–7 (older kids)
Read Revelation 2:1–7 (younger kids)

TODAY'S PRAYER COUNTRY

UNITED ARAB EMIRATES

There are very few believers here. Pray that they will find friendship, discipleship, and encouragement.

WHAT DID I LEARN FROM GOD'S WORD?

_____
_____
_____
_____

MONTHLY PRAYER PROMISE: Deuteronomy 4:29
But from there you will seek the LORD your God and you will find him, if you search after him with all your heart and with all your soul.

WHAT WILL I DO TO OBEY GOD TODAY?

_____
_____
_____
_____
_____
_____
_____
_____

ASIA

FACT
People here are richer than in any other Arab country.

DECEMBER 4

Read Revelation 2:8–11 (older kids)
Read Revelation 2:8–11 (younger kids)

TODAY'S PRAYER COUNTRY

UNITED KINGDOM

Attendance is dropping in many churches. Pray for these churches to become focused on outreach.

WHAT DID I LEARN FROM GOD'S WORD?

_____
_____
_____
_____

MONTHLY PRAYER PROMISE: Deuteronomy 4:29
But from there you will seek the LORD your God and you will find him, if you search after him with all your heart and with all your soul.

WHAT WILL I DO TO OBEY GOD TODAY?

_____
_____
_____
_____
_____
_____
_____

EUROPE

FACT
The United Kingdom consists of England, Scotland, Wales, and Northern Ireland.

DECEMBER 5

Read Revelation 2:12–17 (older kids)
Read Revelation 2:12–17 (younger kids)

TODAY'S PRAYER COUNTRY

UNITED KINGDOM

Teenagers here face very difficult challenges. Pray for them to see Jesus as their only hope.

WHAT DID I LEARN FROM GOD'S WORD?

_____
_____
_____
_____

MONTHLY PRAYER PROMISE: Deuteronomy 4:29
But from there you will seek the LORD your God and you will find him, if you search after him with all your heart and with all your soul.

WHAT WILL I DO TO OBEY GOD TODAY?

_____
_____
_____
_____
_____
_____

EUROPE

FACT
The United Kingdom is a constitutional monarchy and a parliamentary democracy.

DECEMBER 6

Read Revelation 2:18–29 (older kids)
Read Revelation 2:18–29 (younger kids)

TODAY'S PRAYER COUNTRY

UNITED STATES

The US is in need of revival. Pray for American believers to become serious about their commitment to God.

WHAT DID I LEARN FROM GOD'S WORD?

_____
_____
_____
_____

MONTHLY PRAYER PROMISE: Deuteronomy 4:29
But from there you will seek the LORD your God and you will find him, if you search after him with all your heart and with all your soul.

WHAT WILL I DO TO OBEY GOD TODAY?

_____
_____
_____
_____
_____
_____
_____

NORTH AMERICA

FACT
The United States of America is the world's third-largest nation.

DECEMBER 7

Read Revelation 3:1–6 (older kids)
Read Revelation 3:1–6 (younger kids)

TODAY'S PRAYER COUNTRY

UNITED STATES

Thirty-five percent of all foreign missionaries are American. Pray for churches to send even more missionaries.

WHAT DID I LEARN FROM GOD'S WORD?

_____
_____
_____
_____

MONTHLY PRAYER PROMISE: Deuteronomy 4:29
But from there you will seek the LORD your God and you will find him, if you search after him with all your heart and with all your soul.

WHAT WILL I DO TO OBEY GOD TODAY?

_____
_____
_____
_____
_____
_____
_____

NORTH AMERICA

FACT
The first McDonald's restaurant opened in the US in 1955. Now there are 28,000 restaurants in 121 countries.

DECEMBER 8

Read Revelation 3:7–13 (older kids)
Read Revelation 3:7–13 (younger kids)

TODAY'S PRAYER COUNTRY

URUGUAY

Over half the people are connected to the Catholic church but do not have a personal relationship with Jesus Christ. Pray for them to come to Christ.

WHAT DID I LEARN FROM GOD'S WORD?

_____
_____
_____
_____

MONTHLY PRAYER PROMISE: Deuteronomy 4:29
But from there you will seek the LORD your God and you will find him, if you search after him with all your heart and with all your soul.

WHAT WILL I DO TO OBEY GOD TODAY?

_____
_____
_____
_____
_____
_____
_____

SOUTH AMERICA

FACT
Uruguay is the world's second-largest exporter of wool.

DECEMBER 9

Read Revelation 3:14–22 (older kids)
Read Revelation 3:14–22 (younger kids)

TODAY'S PRAYER COUNTRY

URUGUAY

Many false teachings and cults are popular in Uruguay. Pray for the people here to see the truth found in the Bible.

WHAT DID I LEARN FROM GOD'S WORD?

_____
_____
_____
_____

MONTHLY PRAYER PROMISE: Deuteronomy 4:29
But from there you will seek the LORD your God and you will find him, if you search after him with all your heart and with all your soul.

WHAT WILL I DO TO OBEY GOD TODAY?

_____
_____
_____
_____
_____
_____

SOUTH AMERICA

FACT
Uruguay became independent in 1828, after 150 years of Spanish and Portuguese rule.

DECEMBER 10

Read Revelation 4 (older kids)
Read Revelation 4:8–11 (younger kids)

TODAY'S PRAYER COUNTRY

UZBEKISTAN

If you share Christ in this country,
you could get three years in jail.
Pray for faithful witnesses.

WHAT DID I LEARN FROM GOD'S WORD?

_____
_____
_____
_____

MONTHLY PRAYER PROMISE: Deuteronomy 4:29
But from there you will seek the LORD your God and you will find him, if you search after him
with all your heart and with all your soul.

WHAT WILL I DO TO OBEY GOD TODAY?

_____
_____
_____
_____
_____
_____
_____

ASIA

FACT
Uzbekistan is the world's third-
largest producer of cotton.

DECEMBER 11

Read Revelation 5 (older kids)
Read Revelation 5:8–14 (younger kids)

TODAY'S PRAYER COUNTRY

UZBEKISTAN

The government here targets evangelistic churches and makes things rough for them. Pray for this to stop.

WHAT DID I LEARN FROM GOD'S WORD?

_____
_____
_____
_____

MONTHLY PRAYER PROMISE: Deuteronomy 4:29
But from there you will seek the LORD your God and you will find him, if you search after him with all your heart and with all your soul.

WHAT WILL I DO TO OBEY GOD TODAY?

_____
_____
_____
_____
_____
_____
_____

ASIA

FACT
Uzbekistan used to be part of the vast Mongol empire.

DECEMBER 12

Read Revelation 6 (older kids)
Read Revelation 6:1–6 (younger kids)

TODAY'S PRAYER COUNTRY

VANUATU

There are 109 languages in Vanuatu. Pray for people to hear the gospel in their own language.

WHAT DID I LEARN FROM GOD'S WORD?

_____

_____

_____

_____

MONTHLY PRAYER PROMISE: Deuteronomy 4:29
But from there you will seek the LORD your God and you will find him, if you search after him with all your heart and with all your soul.

WHAT WILL I DO TO OBEY GOD TODAY?

_____

_____

_____

_____

_____

_____

_____

AUSTRALASIA

FACT
In 1800, there were about 1 million people in Vanuatu; now there are about 200,000.

DECEMBER 13

Read Revelation 7 (older kids)
Read Revelation 7:9–17 (younger kids)

TODAY'S PRAYER COUNTRY
VANUATU

This nation's motto is "In God We Stand."
Pray that this will be true.

WHAT DID I LEARN FROM GOD'S WORD?

_____
_____
_____
_____

MONTHLY PRAYER PROMISE: Deuteronomy 4:29
But from there you will seek the LORD your God and you will find him, if you search after him
with all your heart and with all your soul.

WHAT WILL I DO TO OBEY GOD TODAY?

_____
_____
_____
_____
_____
_____
_____

AUSTRALASIA

FACT
Vanuatu is made up of about eighty-
three islands in the South Pacific.

DECEMBER 14

Read Revelation 8 (older kids)
Read Revelation 8:1–5 (younger kids)

TODAY'S PRAYER COUNTRY

VATICAN CITY

Pray for Catholics here and around the world to see that Jesus is the only One to pray to for salvation.

WHAT DID I LEARN FROM GOD'S WORD?

_____
_____
_____
_____

MONTHLY PRAYER PROMISE: Deuteronomy 4:29
But from there you will seek the LORD your God and you will find him, if you search after him with all your heart and with all your soul.

WHAT WILL I DO TO OBEY GOD TODAY?

_____
_____
_____
_____
_____
_____
_____

EUROPE

FACT
Vatican City is located in Rome, and the Pope has full legal, executive, and judicial powers.

DECEMBER 15

Read Revelation 9 (older kids)
Read Revelation 9:20–21 (younger kids)

TODAY'S PRAYER COUNTRY

VATICAN CITY

Pray for those who are living in spiritual darkness in Vatican City.

WHAT DID I LEARN FROM GOD'S WORD?

_____
_____
_____
_____

MONTHLY PRAYER PROMISE: Deuteronomy 4:29
But from there you will seek the LORD your God and you will find him, if you search after him with all your heart and with all your soul.

WHAT WILL I DO TO OBEY GOD TODAY?

_____
_____
_____
_____
_____
_____
_____

EUROPE

FACT
A treaty in 1929 between the Vatican and Italy established the autonomy of the Vatican.

DECEMBER 16

Read Revelation 10 (older kids)
Read Revelation 10:1–7 (younger kids)

TODAY'S PRAYER COUNTRY

VENEZUELA

Eighty-five percent of the people are involved in some kind of occult religion or practice. Pray for them to get rid of idols.

WHAT DID I LEARN FROM GOD'S WORD?

_____

_____

_____

_____

MONTHLY PRAYER PROMISE: Deuteronomy 4:29
But from there you will seek the LORD your God and you will find him, if you search after him with all your heart and with all your soul.

WHAT WILL I DO TO OBEY GOD TODAY?

_____

_____

_____

_____

_____

_____

_____

FACT
Venezuela was a Spanish colony until 1811.

DECEMBER 17

Read Revelation 11 (older kids)
Read Revelation 11:1–3 (younger kids)

TODAY'S PRAYER COUNTRY

VENEZUELA

Thousands of children are living in orphanages or on the streets. Pray for these children who have no parents.

WHAT DID I LEARN FROM GOD'S WORD?

_____
_____
_____
_____

MONTHLY PRAYER PROMISE: Deuteronomy 4:29
But from there you will seek the LORD your God and you will find him, if you search after him with all your heart and with all your soul.

WHAT WILL I DO TO OBEY GOD TODAY?

_____
_____
_____
_____
_____
_____
_____

SOUTH AMERICA

FACT
Venezuela is one-third larger than Texas and occupies much of the northern coast of South America.

DECEMBER 18

Read Revelation 12 (older kids)
Read Revelation 12:7–12 (younger kids)

TODAY'S PRAYER COUNTRY

VIETNAM

There are very few churches in the northern part of Vietnam. Pray for more churches to be started.

WHAT DID I LEARN FROM GOD'S WORD?

_____
_____
_____
_____

MONTHLY PRAYER PROMISE: Deuteronomy 4:29
But from there you will seek the LORD your God and you will find him, if you search after him with all your heart and with all your soul.

WHAT WILL I DO TO OBEY GOD TODAY?

_____
_____
_____
_____
_____
_____
_____

ASIA

FACT
Vietnam is the world's second-largest exporter of rice.

DECEMBER 19

Read Revelation 13 (older kids)
Read Revelation 13:1–4 (younger kids)

TODAY'S PRAYER COUNTRY
VIETNAM

Vietnam is one of the world's worst persecutors of Christians. Pray for persecution to stop.

WHAT DID I LEARN FROM GOD'S WORD?

_____
_____
_____
_____

MONTHLY PRAYER PROMISE: Deuteronomy 4:29
But from there you will seek the LORD your God and you will find him, if you search after him with all your heart and with all your soul.

WHAT WILL I DO TO OBEY GOD TODAY?

_____
_____
_____
_____
_____
_____
_____

ASIA

FACT
From 1941 until 1985, Vietnam was continually at war.

DECEMBER 20

Read Revelation 14 (older kids)
Read Revelation 14:1–5 (younger kids)

TODAY'S PRAYER COUNTRY
WESTERN SAHARA

Because of war, there is much conflict in this land. Pray for these people to find the Prince of Peace.

WHAT DID I LEARN FROM GOD'S WORD?

_____
_____
_____
_____

MONTHLY PRAYER PROMISE: Deuteronomy 4:29
But from there you will seek the LORD your God and you will find him, if you search after him with all your heart and with all your soul.

WHAT WILL I DO TO OBEY GOD TODAY?

_____
_____
_____
_____
_____
_____
_____

AFRICA

FACT
Located in northwest Africa, Western Sahara is actually ruled by Morocco.

DECEMBER 21

Read Revelation 15 (older kids)
Read Revelation 15:3–4 (younger kids)

TODAY'S PRAYER COUNTRY

WESTERN SAHARA

The official religion is Islam, and any Muslims converting to Christianity will face persecution. Pray for endurance.

WHAT DID I LEARN FROM GOD'S WORD?

_____
_____
_____
_____

MONTHLY PRAYER PROMISE: Deuteronomy 4:29
But from there you will seek the LORD your God and you will find him, if you search after him with all your heart and with all your soul.

WHAT WILL I DO TO OBEY GOD TODAY?

_____
_____
_____
_____
_____
_____
_____

AFRICA

FACT
In August 2001, former secretary of state James Baker proposed that Western Sahara should become an autonomous region of Morocco.

DECEMBER 22

TODAY'S PRAYER COUNTRY

WALES

Pray for new churches to be started in Wales.

WHAT DID I LEARN FROM GOD'S WORD?

_____

_____

_____

_____

MONTHLY PRAYER PROMISE: Deuteronomy 4:29
But from there you will seek the LORD your God and you will find him, if you search after him with all your heart and with all your soul.

WHAT WILL I DO TO OBEY GOD TODAY?

_____

_____

_____

_____

_____

_____

EUROPE

FACT
Wales lies west of England and is separated from it by the Cambrian Mountains.

DECEMBER 23

Read Revelation 17 (older kids)
Read Revelation 17:14–18 (younger kids)

TODAY'S PRAYER COUNTRY

WALES

Many teenagers in Wales have no hope. Pray for them to find the only source of hope, Jesus Christ.

WHAT DID I LEARN FROM GOD'S WORD?

MONTHLY PRAYER PROMISE: Deuteronomy 4:29
But from there you will seek the LORD your God and you will find him, if you search after him with all your heart and with all your soul.

WHAT WILL I DO TO OBEY GOD TODAY?

EUROPE

FACT
In 1999, Wales became more self-governing than in the last 600 years. In the past, Great Britain governed Wales.

DECEMBER 24

Read Revelation 18 (older kids)
Read Revelation 18:4–8 (younger kids)

TODAY'S PRAYER COUNTRY

YEMEN

It is illegal for Muslims to become Christians here. Pray that the gospel will spread and be heard by everyone.

WHAT DID I LEARN FROM GOD'S WORD?

_____
_____
_____
_____

MONTHLY PRAYER PROMISE: Deuteronomy 4:29
But from there you will seek the LORD your God and you will find him, if you search after him with all your heart and with all your soul.

WHAT WILL I DO TO OBEY GOD TODAY?

_____
_____
_____
_____
_____
_____
_____

ASIA

FACT
Yemen is one of the least evangelized countries in the world.

DECEMBER 25

Read Revelation 19:1–10 (older kids)
Read Revelation 19:1–4 (younger kids)

TODAY'S PRAYER COUNTRY

YEMEN

Pray that there will be opportunities for believers to meet and worship together in Yemen.

WHAT DID I LEARN FROM GOD'S WORD?

MONTHLY PRAYER PROMISE: Deuteronomy 4:29
But from there you will seek the LORD your God and you will find him, if you search after him with all your heart and with all your soul.

WHAT WILL I DO TO OBEY GOD TODAY?

ASIA

FACT
Yemen is about the size of France and is located just south of Saudi Arabia.

DECEMBER 26

Read Revelation 19:11–21 (older kids)
Read Revelation 19:11–16 (younger kids)

TODAY'S PRAYER COUNTRY

ZAIRE

A thousand people die every day here because of starvation and disease. Pray for them to have food and medicine.

WHAT DID I LEARN FROM GOD'S WORD?

MONTHLY PRAYER PROMISE: Deuteronomy 4:29
But from there you will seek the LORD your God and you will find him, if you search after him with all your heart and with all your soul.

WHAT WILL I DO TO OBEY GOD TODAY?

AFRICA

FACT
This country should be wealthy but is actually one of the poorest in the world, and so it is known as "the world's greatest disaster."

DECEMBER 27

Read Revelation 20 (older kids)
Read Revelation 20:1–6 (younger kids)

TODAY'S PRAYER COUNTRY

ZAIRE

At least thirty different translations of the Bible are needed for the people who live in Zaire. Pray for translators.

WHAT DID I LEARN FROM GOD'S WORD?

_____
_____
_____
_____

MONTHLY PRAYER PROMISE: Deuteronomy 4:29
But from there you will seek the LORD your God and you will find him, if you search after him with all your heart and with all your soul.

WHAT WILL I DO TO OBEY GOD TODAY?

_____
_____
_____
_____
_____
_____

AFRICA

FACT
Kinshasa, the capital city, is the largest city in Zaire, with more than 6 million people.

DECEMBER 28

Read Revelation 21:1–8 (older kids)
Read Revelation 21:1–4 (younger kids)

TODAY'S PRAYER COUNTRY
ZAMBIA

In 1991 Zambia was dedicated as a Christian country, but many people have not put their faith in Christ. Pray for them.

WHAT DID I LEARN FROM GOD'S WORD?

_____
_____
_____
_____

MONTHLY PRAYER PROMISE: Deuteronomy 4:29
But from there you will seek the LORD your God and you will find him, if you search after him with all your heart and with all your soul.

WHAT WILL I DO TO OBEY GOD TODAY?

_____
_____
_____
_____
_____
_____
_____

AFRICA

FACT
Zambia is home to Victoria Falls, known as "the smoke that thunders." It is the largest waterfall in the world.

DECEMBER 29

Read Revelation 21:9–27 (older kids)
Read Revelation 21:22–27 (younger kids)

TODAY'S PRAYER COUNTRY
ZAMBIA

Pray for the many people with AIDS who seem to have no hope. They need Jesus Christ to help them.

WHAT DID I LEARN FROM GOD'S WORD?

_____
_____
_____
_____

MONTHLY PRAYER PROMISE: Deuteronomy 4:29
But from there you will seek the LORD your God and you will find him, if you search after him with all your heart and with all your soul.

WHAT WILL I DO TO OBEY GOD TODAY?

_____
_____
_____
_____
_____
_____
_____

AFRICA

FACT
Zambia has the highest level of AIDS orphans in the world.

DECEMBER 30

Read Revelation 22:1–5 (older kids)
Read Revelation 22:1–5 (younger kids)

TODAY'S PRAYER COUNTRY
ZIMBABWE

Pray for this nation that there would be change without violence. Many people do not have jobs and are without hope.

WHAT DID I LEARN FROM GOD'S WORD?

_____
_____
_____
_____

MONTHLY PRAYER PROMISE: Deuteronomy 4:29
But from there you will seek the LORD your God and you will find him, if you search after him with all your heart and with all your soul.

WHAT WILL I DO TO OBEY GOD TODAY?

_____
_____
_____
_____
_____
_____

AFRICA

FACT
In the 1920s, white people (one percent of the population) owned seventy percent of the land.

DECEMBER 31

Read Revelation 22:6–21 (older kids)
Read Revelation 22:17–21 (younger kids)

TODAY'S PRAYER COUNTRY
ZIMBABWE

AIDS is really hurting this country. Pray that there will be a way to stop this deadly disease.

WHAT DID I LEARN FROM GOD'S WORD?

_____
_____
_____
_____

MONTHLY PRAYER PROMISE: Deuteronomy 4:29
But from there you will seek the LORD your God and you will find him, if you search after him with all your heart and with all your soul.

WHAT WILL I DO TO OBEY GOD TODAY?

_____
_____
_____
_____
_____
_____
_____

AFRICA

FACT
In Zimbabwe, over forty percent of the people are under age fifteen.

JANUARY PRAYER REQUESTS

_____

_____

_____

_____

_____

_____

_____

_____

_____

_____

_____

_____

_____

_____

_____

_____

_____

_____

_____

_____

_____

_____

_____

_____

_____

_____

_____

FEBRUARY PRAYER REQUESTS

MARCH PRAYER REQUESTS

APRIL PRAYER REQUESTS

MAY PRAYER REQUESTS

JUNE PRAYER REQUESTS

_____
_____
_____
_____
_____
_____
_____
_____
_____
_____
_____
_____
_____
_____
_____
_____
_____
_____
_____
_____
_____
_____
_____
_____
_____
_____

JULY PRAYER REQUESTS

AUGUST PRAYER REQUESTS

SEPTEMBER PRAYER REQUESTS

OCTOBER PRAYER REQUESTS

NOVEMBER PRAYER REQUESTS

_____
_____
_____
_____
_____
_____
_____
_____
_____
_____
_____
_____
_____
_____
_____
_____
_____
_____
_____
_____
_____
_____
_____
_____
_____

DECEMBER PRAYER REQUESTS